Demons, Dissociation and Deliverance.

Christopher and Nataley Ford

Copyright © Christopher Ford

Demons, Deliverance and Dissociation by *Christopher and Nataley Ford*

ISBN – 978-1-4452-7635-9

Contents

Part 1 – The Spiritual Battle
Introduction	05
Satan's downfall	09
Jesus – The world's rescue plan	14
Satan and his work today	33
How Satan and his demons attack people in today's world	59
Practical tools given by God for ministry	69

Part 2 – Dissociation
Trauma	83
Traumatic experiences	84
Dissociation - a medical analysis	91
Dissociative Identity Disorder – The Christian perspective	96
How does Dissociative Identity Disorder occur?	98
Why does Dissociative Identity Disorder occur?	103
Types of Dissociative Personality	104
Demons and Dissociation	109

Part 3 – Nataley's story — 115

References — 180

Introduction

In the beginning God created the Heavens and the Earth and all was good. God's special creation lived in harmony with its creator and all was well in the world.

Unfortunately things were about to change. The angel Lucifer, ranked along side the arc angel Michael decided to rebel against God his creator. This led to Lucifer being banished from the heavens to earth. Lucifer took with him other angels who sided with him in the rebellion in heaven. Lucifer was renamed Satan and he began his work of undermining God and destroying God's special creation, man.

Since that day a divide has formed between man and God in the form of Sin. Satan and his army of demons have used this to their advantage using ingenious methods of keeping man in a state of sin. Small things like the common distractions of a busy life which keep the focus away from God such as a lack of concentration in prayer, the draw of the internet and television, the pull of non Christian friends to things such as witchcraft and the Occult are just some of the ways Satan has endeavoured to keep man from God. He has even used ignorance within the church to meet his ends. For those who do not personally know God, Satan will throw anything at them to stop them coming into a relationship with their heavenly father.

Despite all of this God provided a rescue plan in the form of his son Jesus who came to earth, remained sinless and died on the cross to take all of our sins away, allowing man to come back to God and be delivered from Satan's schemes.

Satan was defeated on the cross, he knows that and all of his demons know that *'at the name of Jesus every knee will bow' (Philippians 2 v*

10). Despite this, Satan and his demons continue to reap havoc in the world and attempt to draw man away from God.

When demons are in control, a person's life will be subject to devastating events. They may be led down a path in their life which causes personal problems; mixing with the 'wrong' type of people, caught up in crime, caught up in child abuse as either the abused or the abuser, led into a Satanic led cult, be drawn into the web of the occult and may even begin to worship Satan himself. All these things are designed to meet Satan's objectives of keeping man away from God.

Satan and his demons are very subtle and will slowly and quietly edge themselves into a person's life until they have taken control and drawn them away from the knowledge of God's love. A person can become physically and emotionally harmed by the demons. Emotional harm can lead to Dissociation, a condition where a person's soul nature can defragment and new personalities (Alters) form from the fragmented pieces. These personalities although still part of the person's core soul are independent and act separately from the main personality,

The only way for a person to be healed is through the love of Jesus, the acceptance of Jesus into the person's life and the healing that only Jesus can bring.

This study outlines the spiritual battle that we all face, how a person can be demonised, what Dissociation is, the way it affects a person's life and the way to healing through Jesus.

**Part 1
The Spiritual Battle**

Satan's Downfall

In the beginning God created the earth and everything in it (Genesis chapter 1). He placed his special creation, man, in a wonderful garden where God and man could communicate freely and easily. The Bible does not state a great deal of detail about the days before sin entered the world but what we do know is that there was no barrier between God and man. Man was free to talk to God within the garden whenever he chose to and God would respond likewise. Man was created in God's image and both parties enjoyed communing in this special relationship.

Then everything changed. Sin entered the world and disrupted mans special relationship with God. Genesis tells the story of the first temptation that man faced. The tree of knowledge stood at the centre of the Garden of Eden. It was forbidden for Adam and Eve to eat the fruits from the tree. Eve was persuaded by the serpent (which was Satan) to eat from the tree, which she did. Eve also tempted Adam to do the same. At this point they gained all the knowledge that was previously hidden from them. Unknown to Adam and Eve a mighty struggle was taking place in heaven.

Lucifer, an angel of God was ranked amongst the highest in the angel ranks. His status was equal only to the Arc Angel Michael. He was a beautifully created angel and was very close to God. Lucifer was filled with so much pride that he was convinced himself and other like minded and weaker angels that he was equal to God his creator. Lucifer tried to take for himself all the glory that belonged to God.

God would not tolerate this or any other kind of rebellion in the heavenly ranks. A great battle ensued between Lucifer with the angels taken in by his pride, and those good angels that were true to God. Lucifer was expelled from heaven and thrown down to earth along with the angels that fought alongside him. The Bible described the events in the book of Revelation.

> 'And there was war in heaven. Michael and his angels fought against the dragon, and the dragon and his angels fought back. But he was not strong enough, and they lost their place in heaven. The great dragon was hurled down – that ancient serpent called the devil, or Satan, who leads the whole world astray. He was hurled to earth, and his angels with him' (Revelation 12 v 7-9).

In the gospel of Luke, Jesus states that he ' *saw Satan fall like lightning from heaven'* (Luke 10 v18).

As the Bible explains, Lucifer was renamed Satan which means an adversary or the one who opposes (Matthew 4 v10). Due to Satan's frustration at failing to take God's throne, he began to carry out a work of destroying man, Gods special creation. He was determined to put up blockages to the perfect communication that was in existence between man and his creator.

God punished Satan for his rebellion by ordering his expulsion from heaven. Satan will try every means possible to sow that same spirit of rebellion in man in order to keep him away from God. It is his way of reaping revenge on God and spoiling his plans for his creations. For those who do rebel along with Satan they must be made aware of God's promise to Satan when he was thrown down to earth - eternal punishment in the lake of fire for him and all of his followers whether demon or human (*Revelation 20 v 7-15 and Matthew 25 v 41-46)*. It is a terrifying reality for those who do not love God and live under His law.

Throughout the Bible Satan has attacked God's people and tried to take them away from the one who loves them. If we turn to the very beginning of the Bible, as mentioned earlier, the serpent (Satan) tempts Adam and Eve and draws them away from the shelter and protection of God. It was at this point that the world came under the control of Satan. Satan used his free will to oppose God and now sows the seed in the human race so that they will use their own free will against their creator God. This will cause the perfect communion between God and man to irretrievably break down and to never be the same again. At this point sin has entered the world.

From the moment sin entered the world things went drastically wrong for God's people. Everywhere we look within the Bible people were turning to sin. Brother was killing brother *(Genesis 4)*, fighting was breaking out between the tribes of Israel and adultery and homosexuality were commonplace. People were turning to sin and causing disastrous problems within the world that God became so upset that his creation had moved so far away in the relationship that he decided to start again. After choosing a faithful servant and his family to survive along with multitudes of animals on a large boat, God flooded the earth and wiped everything out *(Genesis 6)*.

Even after the flood and the world got back on it's feet, Satan continued to work against God and sow the seed of rebellion in man. It is evident throughout the Bible, and indeed in society today, that Satan uses people's human desires to trap them, and before they realise it they have turned away from God. James writes that *'Evil desire conceives and gives birth to sin, and sin, when it is fully grown gives birth to death'* (James 1 v15). If we take this verse in the context of how Satan works in a person's life, Satan plants a thought in someone's mind (the temptation), if a person acts on that thought it causes them to sin against God. If not repented, the sin can become so large through repeated habitual sin (that is sin that is repeated so frequently that it becomes common and routine in a persons life and becomes a habit. In some cases it could also develop into an addiction. This can be evident through such things as the use of internet pornography, blasphemy and sexual activities outside of a God blessed relationship) that the person becomes spiritually dead and Satan has been successful in his aim to destroy God's special creation.

Due to man's sins through the ages, desires have become inbuilt into the human psyche such as greed and the lust for power and wealth. Satan feeds off these things to continue his rebellion within man. When you break down and analyse the most common sinful acts, they can be split down and divided into categories headed by these three motivators indicated above.

To understand how Satan works we must firstly look at the characteristics of Satan. The Bible provides numerous insights into his character. Detailed here are just a few of the many.(1)

1. He is a created being. God created Satan as an angel to sit alongside and commune with him (*Ezekiel 28 v13-15*). He cannot create anything for himself. The Psalmist states that 'He (God) made man a little lower than the angels' *(Psalm 8 v 5)*. So in the eyes of God, Satan as an angel is only of slightly more value to God than man.

2. Satan is limited in both time and location. He is not omnipresent and needs an army of demons to carry out his work on his behalf *(Job 1 v 6-7)*. His exact location is often not known but he communicates through a network of highly trained and committed demon spirits. Even though he is not at an event himself, he is well informed of what is happening.

---

[1] Adapted from Healing Through Deliverance – The Biblical Basis by Peter Horrobin

3. He does not know everything. He has limited knowledge. He uses his army of demons to gain knowledge; he only knows what his demons can find out and tell him. They are networked to be able to provide this *(Acts 19 v 15)*.

4. Satan's power is limited to what God will allow him to do *(Job 1 v 6-12)*. He is in the same situation as man. Both have power but are unable to work outside of the power that God has delegated to them. God will stop the power given when Satan pushes too much. He is reigned in if he oversteps the mark.

5. He is the god of this world. The earth and fallen man are under his control except of course for those who have turned back to God through Jesus *(2 Corinthians 4 v 4)*. This is allowed by God for the moment. But the day will come when God ceases Satan's reign and banishes him to eternal death.

6. He is the antichrist, the exact opposite to Christ (*1 John 4 v 1-4, 2 John v 7*). He wishes to be the Christ, but that is something that he can never be, so he has set himself up in direct opposition to Christ.

7. He is an accuser and a slanderer *(Revelation 12 v 10, Matthew 4 v 1, and John 8 v 44)*. Satan causes people to sin and then accuses them of the sin causing the sinner to doubt salvation through Jesus Christ.

8. He is a liar *(John 8 v 44)*. He is unable to tell the truth unless being held directly accountable to God. He will tell as many lies as is needed to stop the sinner receiving salvation.

9. He is a murderer as his primary objective is to destroy life. (*John 10 v 10*). He hates God's special creation and will do whatever it takes to wipe it out one soul at a time.

10. He seeks to dominate people and situations *(Acts 10 v 38)*. He uses his demons to go into situations to ensure that God is not thought about and to keep control of the situation and the people involved.

With Satan in control as the 'god of this world', God's special creation is in dire trouble. Humankind has been distracted away from the creator God who loves them into a world of fear and danger where the ultimate end is eternal death. Satan will try everything within his power to ensure he takes as many men with him to the lake of fire (also called the pit) described in the book of Revelation 19 v 20 (we shall look later at the ways in which he entraps people in today's world). But God had a plan to give his special creation a second chance. A get out of jail free card to avoid eternal spiritual death. God chose the ultimate way to restore the relationship between God and man.

Jesus – The world's rescue plan

The country was in such turmoil, there was upheaval everywhere as the governor had called everyone to return to their home town to register in the census. Joseph was returning to his home town of Bethlehem, the town of David with his pregnant teenage wife. It was a special baby that was revealed to Mary, Joseph's wife, by an angel of God. Due to there being no room in any of the inns or houses Mary's baby, Jesus was born in a dirty filth ridden stable amongst the animals *(Luke 2)*.

The thing that made this new addition to the world so special was that he was God's own son, the Messiah, that was prophesied about in the Old Testament; the Messiah the Jews were waiting for to come and save the world; the Messiah the Jewish nation are still waiting for today.

> 'For unto us a child is born, to us a son is given, and the government will be on his shoulders. And he will be called wonderful counsellor, mighty God, everlasting father, prince of peace.' (Isaiah 9 v 6).

God gave the world the ultimate gift - His one and only son. God sent him into the world as a defenceless baby at a time when the world was suffering from major social and political strain. He was sent even though man had turned away from him and was blinded by the works of Satan, God still loved his special creation. God sent his son to fulfil the prophecy of Isaiah, to save the world and reopen the lines of communication between God and man. God knew from the start how Jesus' life would pan out (as he does for all of us), it must have been discussed in heaven before Jesus was sent as a baby to this broken world.

Although many of the world's population had turned away and was now obeying Satan the 'god of this world', Jesus came to earth to give man a second chance to come back to God.

If you read the gospels you will notice that there seems to be a blanket covering much of Jesus' early life on earth until his ministry commences. One incident seems to be of notable value to the writers of the gospels as it gets a mention in more than one. We can assume that this incident has been placed in the gospels to give the reader an early indication of the divinity of Jesus. We read the account of when Jesus was taken by his parents to the temple where he was found by them, teaching the religious men of the day, after going missing. We must make note of how much wisdom and knowledge of the scriptures Jesus exhibits at such an early age - a far superior knowledge to anyone else his age in his day and most probably in the current day and age also.

What we can surmise from this that Jesus had a normal childhood upbringing for the time. He must have learnt his earthly fathers skills and business as a carpenter while living in the countryside. This is evident through his knowledge and demonstration of these things in the examples used throughout his teachings. He would have been given a good grounding which helps him to respond with empathy to those he met during his ministry.

What we do know, and what is evident throughout the gospels is that Jesus came to show people the way back to God through the way he lived his life and taught people about the things of God.

Throughout Jesus' ministry he actively sought to show the kingdom of God to everyone he came into contact with, which caused him to engage in direct spiritual conflict with Satan and his demons on a regular basis. Let's take a look at some key examples from Jesus' life which illustrate the conflict Jesus faced with Satan and the way in which he showed his heavenly fathers kingdom to fallen man.

- *The temptations*

Early on in Jesus' ministry he experienced forty days in the desert wilderness in which time Satan attempted to halt his mission before it started by tempting him. If Satan had succeeded, Jesus' mission would have failed before it had even begun. God's plan to save mankind would have been halted with the possibility of devastating effects.

Jesus had been in this desert wilderness for many days and was getting to be very tired and hungry. Just imagine how Jesus would have felt, he had had no food or drink for many days, endured the desert heat by day, the freezing cold by night with possibly very little sleep due to the hunger pangs eating away at him. He only had his prayers to God his father to rely on. He was facing one of the most extreme endurance tests ever known. When he was feeling at his lowest Satan came to tempt him. We are unsure as to whether Satan came in a physical form to Jesus or whether Satan used constant niggling thoughts inside Jesus as he does constantly with us today. We shall go into the concept of the niggling thoughts later.

Firstly Satan attempted to tempt Jesus by trying to persuade him to make bread to stop his hunger, secondly by offering control of the world if only Jesus would bow down and worship him. In a way, Satan offered Jesus a partnership control of the world. Finally Satan tempted Jesus by encouraging him to throw himself off a cliff so that God's angels could come and save him and prove that he was the Son of God. Each time he was tempted, Jesus resisted and countered the temptations with quotes from the Old Testament. Satan could not find any come back to this so he gave up and left Jesus alone.

This demonstrates to us that it is possible to come into direct conflict with Satan because Jesus himself did. Satan often uses his army of demons who use subtle methods to seduce us into doing the things that will meet his ends. What does this teach us about temptation? Because Jesus was tempted and he resisted, we too can resist temptation from Satan's demons and then they will leave us alone. The Bible states *'resist the devil and he will flee from you'* (James 4 v 7). The Christian must stand firm in his beliefs and hold on to the word of God to keep from being tempted into sin by Satan and his demons.

- *Jesus' battle with the authorities.*

Time and again throughout the gospels we see Jesus confronting both the Jewish and the occupying Roman authorities that were battling for control of the area in which Jesus lived.

An example occurs in Matthew chapter 9. Jesus has just delivered a man of demons and the authorities are outraged that they question his actions and say that he is from the devil. Jesus rebukes them and states that he carries out his ministry through the Spirit of God. We shall look at this story from Matthew in greater detail later.

The Jewish leaders did not like him because he was a radical and they believed that he was threatening their control of the people. They could not see that Jesus had come to fulfil prophecy and they became disgruntled. When they tried to trick him with difficult theological questions he found a true and just answer every time. I am reminded of the time when Jesus was so full of rage that God's house (the temple) was being used as a market place that he turned everything over and destroyed the produce of the stall holders, stating that it was a house of prayer *(John 2 v 12-25)*

The occupying Roman leaders did not like him because he stirred up the people and they were scared that there might be a revolution against their occupation. So they tried their hardest to silence Jesus and his followers. Jesus was not afraid to engage in direct confrontation with the authorities in order for him to show the kingdom of God to the people of his day.

- *Jesus and Deliverance*

Jesus was not afraid to battle Satan's forces and show the kingdom of God throughout his ministry. There are accounts in the Bible that are of note in the study of spiritual warfare and deliverance ministry. It is important to study these and learn the valuable message and learning points that they hold.

We read in Matthew chapter 17 of how a father brought his son to Jesus who had been suffering from seizures, and demons were causing self harm and making the boy fall into a fire. The father had previously asked the disciples to cast out the demon but they were unable as they had doubts over their command from Jesus and their ability to cast out in his name. They were in training and this power was still to come. Jesus cast out the demon because of the father's faith in Jesus and stated that the disciples could not cast it out because their faith was not strong enough.

This passage which appears in three of the gospels *(Matthew 17 v 14-22, Mark 9 v 14-29, Luke 9 v 37-43)* reveals three important points regarding the ministry of deliverance which we should take note of. Firstly, the passage shows that demons can be very violent and can harm their victims if they are left to take hold of the person, grow strong and take complete control. Secondly, demons are no match to the power of Jesus however strong and stubborn they seem to be. Finally, you can only work in the name of Jesus if you believe in Jesus and have the faith to trust in him and believe in the power of Jesus and that it can take the demons out. You have to have total faith and trust in the power of God as if your life depends on it, knowing that at some point in the battle your life may be threatened by a demon and your life will literally depend on your faith. It must be strong. You can be certain that you will overcome because Jesus did. Don't forget that we are more than conquerors through Jesus *(Romans 8 v 28)*. At that point in their lives the disciples lacked the necessary faith to have control over the kingdom of Satan through the name of Jesus. They needed Jesus' help as we do today when we call on the name of Jesus.

We also see in the Bible *(Mark 1 v 21 - 27)* where a man in the synagogue cries out to Jesus saying *'what do you want with us...have you come to destroy us before the appointed time? I know who you are, Holy one of God!'* Jesus discerned that the mans cries were in fact that of a demon inside the man's body. Jesus then commands the demon to be quiet and come out of the man's body. The demons were threatened by the presence of Jesus who was pure and covered with the Holy Spirit. They knew that when they came into contact with him their days inside their host were up.

We learn from this short passage that demons have knowledge, they are aware of what they are doing. Demons know the scriptures and that Jesus has all authority over the demonic world. Satan only has delegated authority which is given to him by God. We also learn that through their knowledge of the Holy Scriptures they know their fate and that there is an appointed time by God for them to go to the pit. This is what they fear. When the demons inside the man are confronted with Jesus they know exactly who he is. They will have heard of him from other demons and they fear him. At his command they have to leave the man's body. Likewise, if a Christian confronts demons in the name of Jesus and is empowered by the Holy Spirit, the demon will know exactly who you are because they have already been warned by other demons in the area. Despite this the demon must leave at your command. The Christian will soon get a reputation and will be known within the demonic kingdom.

The Bible also gives us an insight into the structure of the demonic kingdom. More will be said on this in later sections, but for now if we look at Mark 4 v 35 - 41 we are told of the time when Jesus went across the lake on which he calmed the waters during the storm. Some commentators state that the storm was set by demons to try and prevent Jesus from continuing in his ministry, and to prevent the immediate work that was to be carried out. Once Jesus and the disciples reached the other side of the lake, which was situated next to a graveyard, they were confronted with a demon possessed man that came out of the nearby tombs *(Mark 5 v 1 – 20)*. The demons made the man live in the tombs so that no one would be able to bind them. A demon shouted through the man at Jesus asking what he wanted with him. Jesus then asked his name, which he replied 'Legion'. Within the man were many demons who were working together to control the man.

Legion was a Roman military term for a company of soldiers. A legion of soldiers were highly organised and motivated towards their goal. Although there were a number of men in a legion, they worked together well as a team. They would be highly protected with armour and ensured that they watched each others backs at all times. This shows us that Jesus faced many demons within the man and that they were highly structured and organised. Jesus cast them out and sent them into nearby pigs where they could no longer be of any harm, except for the pigs who ran into the lake and drowned.

When involved with a person in need of deliverance you need to be aware that you may face many spirits within one person, sometimes thousands. They will be working together to keep control of the person and in their current state of bondage. The demonic world is highly organised and needs to be broken down piece by piece. These spirits will have to be taken out systematically. Some will come easily and others will take a long time. Jesus cast the demons out of the man at the same time because the power of God was so concentrated within him that they had no choice but to go at the first time of commanding. As the Christian is not Jesus but his representative on earth, it takes longer to take demons out - taking individual demons or groups of demons bound together out one by one. Do not be disheartened as it does take time and energy to win any battle where lives are at stake.

The gospels also show how Satan can even use the people that we trust to undermine the works of the Kingdom of God. In Mark 8 v 32 - 33, Peter is used by Satan to try and halt Jesus' mission. A demon or Satan himself enters Peter and causes him to rebuke Jesus. The exact words that Peter said are not recorded in the Bible but Jesus recognises what is happening and tells Satan to go. This illustrates that good Christian people in the church can be possessed and cause disruption. Satan uses these people and manipulates them into undermining the work of God and his people in the church, especially those involved in the ministry of deliverance where his territory is at threat the most.

When I first started out and God was revealing his spiritual gifts to me I was becoming aware and involved in the ministry of deliverance. I spoke with my church leader about what was happening at the time as Satan was causing immense problems within my church by possessing and influencing those within it. My minister rebuked me, stated that deliverance was not of God and he did not believe in it and made it so unbearable that I was forced to move church to one more hospitable. When talking about a particular case with a church leader where it was discerned that someone was suffering from a large spirit causing depression, it was identified that deliverance was needed. The church leader stated that demons don't exist and that the person needs the help of doctors and not God. Satan is using God's people, even ministers, to undermine the works of the Kingdom of God even today. Those in ministry must be aware and must take caution but remembering to love those people as God loves them, however hard that may be at the time. The deliverance ministry does not have credibility in the wider church, mainly brought about by fear and ignorance. Those who do not acknowledge the presence of demons and the need for this ministry are falling into Satan's trap . They are submitting to the ruling demon that he has placed on the church. Perfectly good and well meaning Christians need to be aware that they too can fall into this situation if they deny the existence of the supernatural. They are happy to acknowledge the existence of the Holy Spirit but reject any other side in the spiritual battle. The demon over the church needs to be acknowledged and it's power broken for real spiritual growth to develop.

Matthew 12 v 22 - 32 is one of the keynote teachings on the ministry of deliverance in the Bible. It starts with Jesus delivering a man of an evil spirit while the religious teachers were watching. The teachers then question Jesus on what he has just done and state that he is from the devil. Jesus replies that a demon cannot cast out a demon. If so, their house would fall. By this Jesus means that if a demon in one person attempts to take out a demon in another, their network would fall to pieces and come into disarray. It is like a soldier attacking and killing another soldier in his squad while in a combat situation. There would be chaos caused within the ranks with all trust evaporating between the soldier colleagues. Internal inquiries would begin and the troops would not be an effective fighting force. This could then cause the force to lose the battle. It is true that someone who is possessed of demons can appear to cast out a demon from another person but this is not of God. It is used by Satan for his own means. A demon would only cast out another demon in order to gain the trust and confidence from the person. Then at the appointed time, the way is made open for a larger, more powerful demon to enter the person leaving them worse than before the deliverance had taken place. By Jesus stating that their house would fall gives indication of the structure and rank within the demonic kingdom. This statement of Jesus is then backed up by his teaching of the need to bind up the strongman in order to clear out the demons within his control. The strongman is often the most powerful demon within a person. They control and give power to many other demons that are of a lower rank than they are and the lesser demons are used to do their bidding. The strongman can be compared to a commanding officer in charge of a company of soldiers. The commanding officer gives the orders for the soldiers to carry out. The commanding officer remains well protected by his troops at all times and if being attacked, is very difficult to get hold of and is frequently the last man to face before defeating all the troops.

In the passage Jesus states that he casts out demons through the power of the Spirit of God and rebukes the Jewish exorcists who carry out exorcisms under their own means, they may often have demons in themselves which leaves the person in need of deliverance in the state described above. The success rate of the Jewish exorcists was minimal as they were missing a vital ingredient in their ministry.

If you are involved in the ministry of deliverance you must ensure that your own house is in order and that you are under the control of the Holy Spirit. If not, you will do more harm than good to the person that you are ministering to. Pray and seek forgiveness for your sin. Allow the Holy Spirit to bring to your knowledge any hidden and habitual sin. Deal with it in the name of Jesus. Accept Jesus' forgiveness and move on in his work.

I was involved in a ministry session where the church people who represent the body of Christ were invited to pray over the person being ministered to. One of the congregation (a member of the ministry team) was trying to command a demon out but he was getting frustrated that nothing was happening. The person lay on hands but still nothing happened. The person being ministered to became frightened of this person and ran from the church and would only return once he had left. It was later made known that when he laid hands on the person being ministered to a demon transferred from him into the other person causing more problems.

On another visit to the church, the same people came into contact and demons transferred between the two causing further problems for the person being ministered to. This caused a much longer ministry session than originally anticipated as the new demons needed to be taken out first to stop them interfering before the work continued. The sins of the minister were revealed to the one being ministered to through demonic transfer. These sins are still to be addressed and have caused major problems for the deliverance ministry within the church.

The final example that we should consider is found in Matthew 15 v 21 - 28. This is another example of how great faith overcomes Satan and his demons. The passage talks of the great faith of a mother and how through her faith in Jesus her daughter was delivered of a demon by Jesus from a distance. Through the faith in Jesus of a parent, the same can be done today. If a demon states that there are some of it's kind within a child, the parent can take authority over the child in the name of Jesus and the demon can be taken out even if there is a distance between the parent and the child. The spiritual realm is not restricted by time and space so distance is no obstacle.

- *The personal characteristics of Jesus.*

So what makes up the character of Jesus? What makes him stand out from the crowd and fit to carry out God's mission of showing his special creation the Kingdom of God and opening the door to a fresh relationship with his creator.

1. Jesus is the Son of God. It was made known to Mary before his birth that he was a holy child and the one who was to redeem the nation. Throughout Jesus' early life he knew that his father was God and that he was to carry out his mission.
2. Despite this knowledge, Jesus was also human with human weaknesses. He experienced the same human emotions that we all do. He suffered the same heartaches and experienced the same joys. He knew exactly how people felt and was able to connect on the same level as those that he came into contact with.

3. Jesus was kind, loving and merciful.
4. Jesus was strong willed. He knew what was right and what was good for man to enable him to join him in the kingdom of God.
5. Jesus knew his mission on earth and was determined to fulfil it whatever the cost.

Despite Jesus, the Son of God, walking on the earth showing man the kingdom of God, Satan thought that he was in control and was still getting the upper hand through his seed of rebellion despite the defeats of his demons when they came into contact with Jesus. Everything was about to change. Jesus' mission was reaching it's climax and was to signal the beginning of the end for Satan and his kingdom of darkness and herald the beginning of a new chapter for God's special creation.

- *Jesus' death.*

When Jesus rode into Jerusalem heralded as a king he knew that the climax of his mission on earth had started. He knew that within a few days the way to a full relationship with his heavenly father would be open and Satan's kingdom would be defeated forever. For this reason he began to prepare himself and his disciples.

In the evening of Passover, Jesus and his followers met in the house of a man sympathetic to the cause of Jesus to eat the Passover meal together. While the meal was taking place, Jesus gave the disciples a hint of what was to come in the coming hours. Jesus broke bread as a sign of his body broken for all man and they drank from a cup which symbolised his blood. This act that has come to be known as Holy Communion has become an important part of the preparation for any spiritual battle. It enables the partaker to receive the blood of Jesus internally and provide purification of the mind and spirit. It also provides protection for the oncoming battle. Jesus also stated that one of the group was going to betray him. Jesus already knew that Satan had already got to Judas and turned him away from Jesus.

After the meal, Jesus went to a garden to pray *(Luke 22 v 39-46)*. This prayer verbalises his acknowledgement of his final task of his mission. Jesus wrestled with his father throughout the prayer, showing his human side. He asked for a final way out and pleaded for God to choose another way. But Jesus was sure of his mission and what needed to be done for the Kingdom of God that he accepted what was about to happen.

Towards the end of this time of prayer, the Jewish authorities arrived with Judas to arrest Jesus *(Luke 22 v 47-53)*. Judas kissed Jesus as a sign to show the authorities which man to arrest. Although the disciples initially put up a fight leading to one man's ear being sliced off in a vicious battle, Jesus went without a fight and accepted his fate. The disciples split up and went their separate ways before they were also arrested.

In the next few hours Jesus was subjected to the worst humiliation and abuse that anyone could experience at the hands of his captors. He was taken to Pilate, the Roman governor who could find no case against him although the Jewish authorities wanted him killed, so he ordered Jesus to be flogged.

Again the Jewish authorities came to Pilate for Jesus to be killed and again Pilate could not find any case against Jesus amidst tremendous pressure from the Jewish authorities.

Again Pilate could not find any case against Jesus amidst tremendous pressure from the Jewish authorities. Pilate thought of a get out plan which would have dissolved any responsibility that he would have had for killing an innocent man. He would let the people decide. Every year at Passover, the Romans set free one political prisoner. This year the people would have a choice, Jesus an innocent man with no real charges set against him or Barabbas, a convicted murderer. With a little coaxing, the people cried out for Barabbas to be set free sealing Jesus' fate. Death by crucifixion, the most horrendous death that the Romans would inflict on their criminals.

Jesus was stripped and forced to wear a crude robe and a crown made of thorns that ripped into his head by a mocking group of Roman guards. He was then led out of the city where only a few days earlier he was welcomed as a king to the local rubbish heap which was used for executions. There nails were hammered into his hands and feet to secure him to the wooden cross. A sword was also rammed into his side to inflict greater pain and damage on his already broken body.

As the sky turned black, Jesus hung there on the cross with two criminals dying a slow and painful death. As he drew his last breaths he said to his father in heaven *'it is finished....Into your hands I commit my spirit'* (Luke 23 v 46). Signalling that Jesus' mission on earth was finally over.

Because Jesus was sinless, amazing things happened at this point in the spiritual world. When Jesus died he took the punishment for everyone's sins which meant that for everyone who claims God's forgiveness, they would avoid the eternal death that Satan and his demons were dragging people down to.

At the point of Jesus' death, his blood became extremely powerful in the spiritual world. As he hung there on the cross, his blood spilling everywhere, it was also supernaturally spreading throughout the spiritual world. This means that anyone who claims protection through the blood of Jesus will be covered in the righteous, pure blood and no demon can touch them. Demons become greatly harmed if they come into contact with Jesus' blood, hence this is one of the things that they fear above all others. We will look in more detail at the power of the blood of Jesus later.

Another greatly symbolic event took place while Jesus was hanging on the cross. In the Jewish temple, there was an area called 'the holy of holies' where it was said that God was resident. It was barred from public view by a curtain. The High Priest was only allowed in this area once a year to commune directly with God. No other person was ever allowed in this area. As Jesus hung on the cross, the curtain covering this area was torn in two symbolising that the barrier between man and God had been broken down and that God was now accessible to all who wanted to commune with him. The rebuilding of the special relationship had begun.

Jesus died to take the punishment for everyone's sins. Because of this fact Satan can no longer condemn people to eternal death. Whoever calls on the name of the Jesus will be saved from this. Satan is defeated at the cross. He no longer has total control of man. The only control that Satan has over a person is that which the person consciously allows. Once a person chooses to accept God's forgiveness, Satan must give up the control he has previously been allowed to have although this may come as a struggle. The communication lines between man and it's loving creator which he tried his hardest to destroy had been reopened and could never be closed again, however hard he would try. Satan knows that if someone turns back to a loving relationship with God, he has lost the battle for that person's soul and has to give up any rights he has to that person. Jesus died to become the way for man to come back to God. If you believe in Jesus as Son of God, the way to God is open. Jesus now sits with God in heaven looking after each and every one of us.

But Jesus' death is not the end of the story. Three days after the crucifixion, Jesus conquers death by coming back to life completing

God's redemption plan for mankind. This means that Jesus is alive now and for all time. Satan has no power over him, and likewise has no power over those who believe in Jesus and live in the Spirit of God protected by the blood of Jesus.

While writing this section I am staggered once more of how God loves us. So much that he let his own Son go through this horrible and dangerous mission for the sake of mankind. How many of us could say we could do that? I have recently become a father for the first time. My little boy is defenceless; he looks on his parents to provide everything. We have our hopes and dreams for him; I know that the last thing I would wish for him would be to go through a horrific death at an early age to take the punishment for someone else when he was entirely innocent of any crime. What parent would? But that is exactly what God did. It was agreed in heaven before Jesus came that this is what the mission was and God would not intervene at any point, however hard the mission would become. God loved us so much and wanted our love so much in return that he was willing to do this, despite the pain he would have felt as he viewed the events unfolding. Just remember these words:

> *For God so loved the world that he gave his one and only Son. Whoever believes in him shall not perish but have eternal life. For God did not send His Son into the world to condemn the world, but to save the world through him. Whoever believes in him is not condemned, but whoever does not believe stands condemned already because he has not believed in the name of God's one and only Son.* (John 3 v 16-18)

- *The power of the blood of Jesus.*

On Good Friday, Jesus met his end. He fulfilled the Old Testament prophecies by dying to save mankind. His physical body died and his spirit went to heaven. It was at this point that the living blood of Jesus was spilt. This blood is feared by the demonic world because any demon that comes into contact with it becomes severely harmed and can die the second death as described in the book of Revelation. If covered in the living blood of Jesus, demons lose all power.

When deliverance ministers pray the blood of Jesus to wash over a person, it has been known for the demon to cry out in fear because they see the blood as warm and living and they know they will die when they come into contact with it.

Jesus died and at the point of his death, his blood was spilt out and the victory over Satan and the demonic world was taken. When we pray in the Lord's name and through the blood of Jesus against the demonic world, we will win because Jesus has already won for us. We have to exercise our spiritual authority over them.

The story does not end with Easter and the conclusion of Jesus' mission on earth. When Jesus returned to heaven, God gave the disciples a gift to help them with the ongoing mission of showing God's kingdom to fallen man. The day of Pentecost heralded the birth of the church and with this, the gift from God promised to the disciples by Jesus, the Holy Spirit. It came to the disciples as they met and waited in a secret upper room. On this day, the Holy Spirit ministered to the disciples giving them supernatural gifts to proclaim the gospel of Jesus Christ.

From this day the disciples were given the commission to spread the good news of Jesus, to heal the sick and to cast out demons. The authority over the demonic world that belonged to Jesus was passed on to them to exercise in his name and subsequently, many generations on, to us as the present day disciples.

- *The final battle – Revelation*

At the end of the Bible lies a vivid prophecy of the end of this age, where the final battle between the forces of Satan and God takes place. A vicious battle between good and evil takes place and the end of the demonic world is shown. As we look into the pages of Revelation we can see that much of the description of that society can be paralleled to our own. Many are turning away from God and choosing the 'god of this world'. They are building their life on witchcraft, mysticism, new ageism, false teachings and religion and the forming of a secular society that gives no regard to the things of God. It is our job as Christians to show the light of God to them before it is too late and they are on the wrong side of the battle and live eternally in hell.

> 'Then the angel showed me the river of the water of life,
> as clear as crystal, flowing from the throne of God and
> the lamb down the middle of the great street of the city.
> On each side of the river stood the tree of life.'
> (Revelation 22 verse 1 and 2a)

I have had the experience of talking and praying with a person that was severely oppressed. After praying for the Lord's protection, they have dreamed of fire and the river of life as described at the end of the book of Revelation. They relayed to me of the fear that the evil spirit has of this and that they are constantly being told to stay away. The person concerned had never read the book of Revelation and I believe that God directly intercepted the dreams in order to take control of the situation and bring about the deliverance of that person.

Satan and his work today

To understand how Satan works in today's world, let's first look at how he worked in the times recorded in the Bible.

Satan has always been the master of deception. He has used ever increasing and complex ways to trap man and turn him away from a relationship with God. Many of the methods used such as witchcraft, spiritualism, cults, false religions and the basic distractions of life which are all around us today are evident in the Bible and were a successful method of creating a barrier between man and God.

It is important to note that while Satan has developed structures such as those described, the basic distractions found in life are also frequently used in an aim to turn minds away from God. These distractions include such things as causing a lack of concentration when praying, reading the scriptures or talking about the things of God. You must also consider television programmes and the general busyness of life as distractions. If Satan can keep you busy during the day on the routine things, God soon gets pushed to the sidelines.

As previously mentioned, witchcraft is not a new phenomena, it dates back as long as time has been recorded. Throughout the Bible we find examples of where magic has been used by the Pagans of the day against God's people but in every example we will see where the power of God has been far greater and has turned around the evil of magic for his purposes.

If we go right to the beginning of the Bible we will see in Exodus 7 where the Pharaoh was testing Aaron to see if his God had power. The Pharaoh then tried to go one better than Aaron by the use of magicians and sorcerers. God proved that His power was far greater.

> '......Aaron threw his staff down in front of Pharaoh and his officials and it became a snake. Pharaoh then summoned the wise men and sorcerers and the Egyptian magicians also did the same thing by their secret arts. Each one threw down his staff and it became a snake. But Aaron's staff swallowed their staffs.' (Exodus chapter 7)

Throughout the Bible, God is in direct opposition to the evil forces displayed through magical powers. In Ezekiel God says;

> 'I am against your magic charms with which you ensnare people like birds and I will tear them from your arms; I will set free the people you ensnare like birds.' (Ezekiel 13 v 20)

Daniel chapter 2 tells us the story of king Nebuchadnezzar's dream. The king summoned up the wise men of the country that consisted of magicians, enchanters, sorcerers and astrologers so that he could have an interpretation of his dream. The king then threatened them with death if they failed to give him a correct prediction but promised them wealth and gifts if they were correct. They decided that they were unable to fulfil the king's request so he sent out a decree to kill all the educated men within the kingdom.

Through the power of God, Daniel interprets the dream and gives God the glory. Daniel says to the king 'no wise man, enchanter, magician or diviner can explain to the king the mystery he has asked about, but there is a God in heaven who reveals mysteries.' Daniel then reveals to the king that what he saw was the future as God had planned it.

Only God knows the true outcome of events. Predictions through magic and other mystical sources are never true predictions and will all prove to be wrong.

A New Testament reference to magicians appears in Acts with the brief story in chapter 8 of Simon the Sorcerer who used his powers for entertainment, popularity and wealth. He had many followers and thrived on the praise. After hearing a sermon preached by Phillip he was baptised by the Holy Spirit, gave up his magical ways and followed Jesus Christ. Yet again giving us a biblical example of how the power of God can overcome evil in a person's life and completely transform them for good.

If we look at the very end of the Bible, we can see that the magical arts are going to play a large part in the end of the world. Those who repent of the acts will be saved from eternal death and taken to heaven. Those who do not will be punished and given over to Satan.

> *'Nor did they repent of their murders, their magic arts, their sexual immorality or their thefts.'* (Revelation 9 v 21).

> *' He who overcomes will inherit all this, and I will be his God and he will be my son. But the cowardly, the unbelieving, the vile, the murderers, the sexual immoral, those who practice magic arts, the idolaters and all liars – their place will be in the fiery lake of burning sulphur. This is the second death.'* (Revelation 21 v 7 & 8)

God can do marvellous things with the lives of the people he loves and created. He can make even the worst sinner pure. We can look all through the history of mankind to see the power of God transforming the lives of those whom he touches.

Satan and his demons use many devices to entrap mankind and keep them in bondage and away from a loving relationship with God. Some are major ideologies with organised structures and others are a lot more subtle. Every one of these devices is equally dangerous and can open a doorway within a person's soul for a demon to enter their life.

Satan has always aspired to be God and to take his throne. For this reason he has developed his own supernatural gifts that are given to his followers. These are counterfeit gifts that are not of God's creation and are designed to trap people into turning away from God, either denying the existence of God or worshiping Satan. These gifts are evident through the magic arts and especially through spiritualism. Either way, Satan has the person trapped. On the other hand, the supernatural gifts given by God through the Holy Spirit are developed and given to help the Christian, not to hinder or trap them.

There are many ways in which Satan intervenes and brings bondage to the human soul. Methods designed to open up doorways for his demons to enter are:

1. Witchcraft and the Occult – These ancient arts are designed and used by Satan to show power through his counterfeit miraculous signs. A person involved in witchcraft is heavily demonised (has many evil spirits within them) and these demons are in control of the person. They lead the person to believe that they are in fact carrying out the acts. This can be heavily linked with Satanism (or Satanic led cults) which is the worship of Satan himself. Satanism uses rituals and rites to praise Satan and keep him happy. Sexual magic is very dangerous and is quite prominent in today's society. This can

be used to take advantage of people and could lead to rape. There are specific demons involved in the control of a person involved in sexual magic and whole industries have been built up around it. Users of sexual magic are led to use such things as tantric sex and are known to astral project, sometimes across continents to carry out these acts.

2. False religions – Many new religions have sprung up over the years used by Satan to take the focus away from Jesus. Many dangerous cults have also come into existence which is heavily demon led. We have seen in the news in recent years how cults, based on false teachings of the leaders have imprisoned the followers. Some have led to mass suicides by the members believing that they are going to heaven.

3. Mental illness and the mental health industry – Don't get me wrong, I am not saying that all mental illness is created by demons and that psychiatrists are demon led. I mention it as a way into a person's soul that could be abused by demons. When ministering, awareness is needed as to what is true mental illness and what is demon induced. This being said, strong demons can use a person's health problems for their advantage causing them to get addicted to medication and into a cycle that they cannot get out of. Demons use this as a form of bondage as ensure that the person cannot find a way out. In some circumstances, demons can replicate the symptoms of the illness so that the sufferer feels that they are not getting any better and contrive to take more and more addictive medication.

4. Internet – This is being increasingly used by demon led people to entrap through various occult and sexually orientated websites. This quite often targets the young and vulnerable.

5. Abuse – This is frequently used by demons to enter a person's soul. Sexual, physical, emotional and mental abuse are all used in this way. This will be discussed further in the section on Dissociation.

6. Cutting – When a person finds themselves in the emotional state of wanting to cut themselves, demons enter through the cuts. This is heavily linked to illnesses such as depression and occult activity. This could also lead to suicide attempts.

7. Media – We are finding increasingly violent DVD's, video games and music in our shops aimed at young people. Demons use these to indoctrinate young people and get a foothold into their lives to entrap them and lead them into more dangerous pursuits such as the Occult and witchcraft.

8. Gossip – Especially within the church of God. It causes people to turn away from the church and eventually live without God. Satan loves discouraged and inactive Christians as this leads to a divided church.

There are three areas we need to look at in the process of identifying demonic activity within a person. They could have a slight interest in demonic practices or they could be demonic obsessed, where they have an unhealthy interest in the activities of the demonic world. For example, some young people that I know confess to being Satanists without knowing what that exactly entails. They have an interest in magic and Satanic rituals, get hyped up on violent video's, wear all the right clothing, listen to appropriate music but that is as far as it goes. Satan has woven a lie to them saying that this is attractive and their interest grows. Satan has a small foothold into the person's life. They are obsessed by these practices. Satan uses these interests to entrap them further and eventually possess them.

This obsession may be found with impressionable young people that began to watch popular television programmes on subjects such as vampires and witchcraft. They begin to get completely hooked on the programme that they start reading the accompanying books, dressing the same as the characters in the programme and study the subjects identified in more detail. That may be as far as it goes for the majority. Some will take it a stage further and act upon what they see and this is when the situation begins to become dangerous.

Satan begins to increase his claim as the mild interest grows. The person experiments with things of the dark world and widen the already open door into their lives. At this stage they can become demonically oppressed. This is when the pressure increases. Evil thoughts can enter their heads and start to be controlled. Evil spirits bombard them and if they are not strong things can continue to get worse as they are blinded by Satan's lie. So much pressure can be put on the person to comply with the spirits desires that they can become very afraid. Many of these bully tactics occur at night as that is when evil spirits act. They love the darkness because it covers up their deeds and the light threatens them, lack of sleep can occur. We are at our most vulnerable at night and it is harder to defend ourselves. The fear can lead to physical problems such as crying out and wetting the bed due to intense nightmares that they cannot wake from. In extreme circumstances, personal injury may occur in the form of self harming.

The final stage is demonic possession, where evil spirits can be given entrance into the person's body. They can then begin to take control of that person and cause destruction within their life. It is important to note that this can only occur if the person gives the demon a right to enter their lives. When a person is demonically possessed, they may be seen to have supernatural strength that they can't control. All of the bodily functions could be taken over and then the host could have no control over what happens to them when the spirit comes to full consciousness. Demons are rarely at full consciousness all of the time. They are usually deep down in the person's soul and only come to the surface when threatened or called to face judgement by God. They continue their work by subtly putting thoughts into the person's mind in order to keep their control. I have experienced this while on mission in Latvia where one of the street children which the mission team were working with was acting in a very violent manner towards a member of the team. At the mention of Jesus his anger increased and became very violent. After praying for him within the group, he was delivered of the evil spirit and he became a loving and caring affectionate boy instantly. I experienced this again while in America. A lady with many demons was being ministered to and she had to be restrained while the minister cast out the demon. Each time a demon came to consciousness she became out of control and had to be restrained until the rights were identified, repented of and the demon cast out.

Christians need to be aware of the havoc that Satan is causing in our world, the trouble that people are getting into and the fact that they need deliverance. Without us there is no hope for a needy world.

To understand what Satan and his demons are doing within a person's life, we first of all need to identify the root cause of the problem. Observing the persons actions could identify this, but it may not be a complete give away by their actions. Demons can be cunning, just remember that they are in the control of the ultimate deceiver. This is where spiritual discernment is essential. It is important to know if the person is or has been involved in any possible Occult activity, Satanism, witchcraft, idol worship or whether their life is centred on material things. If someone approaches you for help, these questions can then be asked directly. It is important to identify all possible reasons why doors could have been opened within the persons life.

A less obvious cause may be through the activity of past generations of their family. Has there been any history of these types of activities in the generational line? The person being questioned may not know this but any generational involvement will be identified by the demons themselves through the deliverance ministry session. Curses can be made by previous generations in the family line through Occult rituals which can be passed down the generational line. This is evident in those members of the Freemasons and other secret organisations where certain rituals lead to curses being laid on the person and their family which can then be passed to the next generation. This of course can be broken and the person can be set free.

To break a generational curse, firstly it needs to be identified when the curse originated, which family member was originally cursed or laid the curse, and what act caused it. This may be known by the person or it may be necessary to question the demon who holds the rights to the person through the curse in order to identify the details. Once identified, the person being ministered to must confess the sin of the curse, ask and receive God's forgiveness. This will always be received and the right taken away from the demon. The demon can then be taken out of the body and sent to the pit.

Generational curses are a bigger problem than what is widely thought. The person creating the curse may not even know what they are doing and pass it down to the next generation. This is found through the rituals used in Freemasonry. Those going through the initiation ceremony are often unaware of the satanic implications. They are quite often joining for business reasons or because their father and grandfather have been members.

Unfortunately there are those who lay curses on family members for a reason. This is frequently evident with those who take part in serious Occult activities and those involved in cults. They do this in order to keep future generations hooked and involved.

It must be remembered that all generational curses can be broken through the power of Jesus. Once broken, the delivered person and all future generations are free of the curse.

If a person is demonic obsessed, this can be turned around quite easily through education. It may be that a young person may simply grow up and change their attitude and Satan can begin to lose his grip. Although deliverance from this will not be complete until the person comes to Jesus. Deliverance from this obsession will constitute the confessing of sins that have been committed and receiving forgiveness to close any doors that may have been opened. They then need to change their lifestyle and live life in the light of God. At the point of confession and receiving forgiveness it will be important to carry out a spiritual check to ensure that there are no demons dwelling within the person. If it is found that there are, these can be dealt with easily.

In the case of demonic oppression and possession things can get a little more complicated as direct involvement by demonic activity occurs in the person's life. In order to identify the signs of demonic oppression, you need to be aware of such activity as:

- A total rejection of any belief in a loving God which can lead to evil thoughts, non Christian ideas, a hatred of the Bible and those who confess to be Christians. The person may even stop associating with any Christians, causing a breakdown in relationships and a shift in the persons group of friends.

- A restlessness and lack of inner peace. This cannot be fulfilled by worldly things, however much they try. They will not be able to find any peace wherever they turn unless it is back to a relationship with God.

- Paranoia. A sense that people are watching them and plotting against them. This can also be a mental illness.

- A sense that someone else is with them. This may be a manifestation of someone that only they can see. This spirit could put a lot of pressure on them to comply with the ways of Satan and blind them from the truth of God. It may tell them lies such as 'God does not care about you' and 'I'm your god now...follow me'. Not to be mistaken with Schizophrenia, which is a genuine mental illness, although demons can use Schizophrenia for their own means. They can also be convinced that there is genuine Schizophrenia when in fact the problem is purely demonic.

- A wanting to hurt themselves for a reason they don't seem to know.

- An inability or unwillingness to pray or say the name of Jesus. They may also not be able to write or think the name of Jesus without a struggle.

These features are also found in demonic possession but they can also include:

- A change in physical appearance which can include the body wasting away or pains in the body that are not connected to any known illness that the person may have. They may have an evil or frightening expression on their face. Shadows may be cast over the face or the body and in extreme circumstances they may have a shadow that does not resemble their own body. It is almost always the case that spiritual discernment is needed to identify many of these.

- They will not be able to hold any conversations with Christians or about Christian matters without getting very agitated, which could cause screaming and cursing because they find it unbearable. It has been known that the person may get so worked up that they can cry out the name of Satan in the same way as Christians call on the name of Jesus. This is usually the demon responding rather than the affected person.

- They may completely withdraw into themselves. They may wish to have no contact with other people and go into a hermit like state.

- When being prayed for they may go into a trance and find themselves unable to answer any questions because their speech has been bound and the demon has come up to full consciousness. This can also occur with oppression. They will not remember anything when it is over. It may also be the case that the demon makes them act foolish in order to put others off. I have known situations where Holy Communion is being taken and a person being ministered to has become foolish, laughing and pouring the cup of juice over the floor. The demon causing this was severely reprimanded before being cast out.

- They may show supernatural and psychic powers such as clairvoyance and extra strength. This is an extreme circumstance, It all depends on what doors have been opened and what type of demons are in occupation.

Notice how in every situation that is experienced, the demon always acknowledges the presence of God and is scared of the name of Jesus and the cross, even though they may put on a hard front at first by being rude and disrespectful. But this soon stops and the fear comes when faced with the full power of God. Why then are we humans so unsure of the existence of God? We believe in spiritual things now more than ever in the history of mankind but the majority will not accept that God does exist and wants to love them. Unfortunately the spiritual things that our society craves are met by the things made attractive and freely available by Satan. The church is failing our society by not actively showing the kingdom of God to everyone that it meets.

- *Witchcraft*

It is important to identify that witchcraft is a Pagan art which means that those who practice it do not believe in any kind of god and that they worship life forces. These forces being wind, earth, fire and water. They manipulate these forces for their own ends. They tend to attract immature people because it is a forbidden activity and it is often very dangerous, causing it to be a thrill to those who stumble upon it and are attracted to it. They acknowledge good and evil and the power linked with both. 'Black magicians' use magic for evil and controlling purposes while 'white witches' tend to use their powers to supposedly help the magician and the situation that they are involved in. Cursing is often used which can alter a person's state of mind. If a curse has been laid on a person, a severe amount of damage can be caused in the person's life. Damage can also be caused if someone believes that they have been cursed. Discernment is needed to find true cases. Curses are thoughts, proposed actions or pre-planned and determined chants that are manipulated by demons into existence, causing severe pain and suffering on the person who has had the curse laid upon them, until it is repented of and lifted.

All witchcraft is wrong because it is not of God. It is one of the counterfeit gifts that Satan has given the world in opposition to God's spiritual gifts. God's power always rules.

- *Occultism*

An Occultist does not worship anything. Their ideology and powers are based on a mixture of science and witchcraft which manipulates the state of mind. Occult activity includes mediums, palmistry, séances and Ouija boards. Demons are clearly behind all of these activities pulling the strings to fool the person practicing and then to keep them hooked.

- *Satanism*

Satanism is set up in direct opposition to God. Followers worship Satan and believe that Jesus was just sent to put a spanner in the works of Satan's master plan to conquer the world. Satanists hate and despise the church of God on the surface, with one of their symbols being an inverted cross meant as mockery towards Jesus. Deep down many true Satanists will fear it because they know of the power that it holds and that it is far greater than they will ever have or can possibly dream of having.

Satanists practice the powers of extra sensory perception, levitation, psycho kinetic's and can often have out of body experiences. This can include astral projection where a participant's spirit leaves their body and travels to another person with the view of direct communication, often using sexual magic. This can be achieved over any distance. A common activity will be to undergo group hypnosis that summon up demons and leaves the participants mentally and spiritually ruined. This is also a cult practice as cults also take part in Occult activities.

- *Cults*

These groups are set up on false doctrine, sometimes taking a part of Christian doctrine and using it in a twisted, out of context form. Members of the cult often worship the leader, founder or a mythical being or god. They follow the practices set out by the leader of the cult. These practices are ungodly and leave the member of the cult spiritually damaged with many demons. Controlling devices are often placed in the member. The leader controls the members, often brain washing them, offering them great things while undertaking a reign of power and control over them. The acts undertaken by the cults can include rituals, sexual acts, acts of severe violence and mass suicides.

There are hundreds of cults in existence today, some with semi respectability like the Freemasons, Scientology (which had it's awareness risen by popular Hollywood actors becoming members) and Christian Science. Lesser known cults include Children of God, which will be talked about further in part three, to smaller cults which end abruptly with mass suicide on the promise that they will go to heaven. Often the leader flees the cult at this point and survives. All cults are Satanic led as they are not of God and are influenced by demons.

Cults are very possessive of their members. If one leaves or tries to escape the cult will go to any means necessary to get the member back, even resorting to kidnapping. It is very dangerous work for those who are in the work of rescuing cult members from their grips. It could become a life threatening work as the cult will do anything they can to stop it.

- *Devices*

It has been known for satanic cults to implant objects in the body in order to control a member. This is done supernaturally through demons. These devices include tracking devices so that the cult always knows where the members are even if the member leaves. They are used to locate them at a later date if they wish to blackmail them. They are also used for groups of demons to find each other and give each other access to the host. Due to these tracking devices, it can be almost impossible for a member to leave a cult. If a former cult member comes for deliverance, these objects need to be spiritually burned with holy water to render them inactive.

Spiritual seeds can also be placed in the body by a strong demon to enable itself to reproduce and strengthen its hold on the host.

Cursed objects such as jewellery can also be used for the same purposes of keeping hold of cult members. It has also been known for demonically led members of the military and the healthcare professions to implant devices into new recruits and patients.

These are the things that we as Christians face in our society today. These are the realities of the spiritual war that we are involved in. We are in a battle for a person's soul on behalf of God. The threat is large but God has given us the tools to successfully deal with what is thrown at us from Satan. We need to strengthen our spiritual gifts so that our armour and our battle plans become stronger. Continue to pray, grow in Christ and accept the blessings and gifts that he gives us so that we become better equipped for the tasks ahead of us.

It is known that some people who are oppressed or possessed can be attracted to a Christian for help. They can sometimes see something in the eyes of the Christian in certain situations. For example, when I talk to people who are suffering from some sort of spiritual oppression, they say that when we talk about the situation, the spirit manifestation appears to them and provokes fear within the person, but something appears in my eyes which renders the spirit powerless to act and the person feels comfortable and safe while it is there. It is a mystery to me what exactly is in the eye, but I believe that God has put it there as part of the gifts that he has given me.

Many different types and groupings of spirits can affect people. There are sixteen different groupings of evil spirits that have been identified. We shall look at each one in turn. At this point we must note that demons take on their own name but despite the name it has given itself, it can be categorised into one of the groupings identified below which gives insight into their actions. The name taken by each demon is often representative of the situation leading to it's entry into the person's soul.

- Spirits of divination

The dictionary definition of divination is 'the practice of attempting to foretell future events or discover hidden knowledge by occult or supernatural means.'

The types of action carried out by these spirits are very common in our modern society. It includes fortune telling, sorcery, hand writing analysis, star gazing and horoscopes, hypnosis, water witching, divination and magic.

Satan is using this type of spirit a lot in our modern society. How easy is it to read our horoscope or receive a zodiac reading. We only have to look in our morning newspaper to have a daily forecast presented to us. Hypnosis and psychics are common on our television screens and many psychic fairs are becoming evident within our society. I was looking through the local newspaper this morning which is given away free at train stations.

While flicking through, I found half a page of small advertisements for spiritual readings. Many of the readings come at a price, one even stated that you had the reading today and then you wait two weeks for the results.

We as Christians know that the only source of truth about the future is from God and that it is a sin to gain knowledge in any other way than when it is presented in some way to us by God. We must live in faith and trust in God for the future, leaving whatever he has planned in his hands.

This type of spirit is evident within the Bible *(Acts 16 v 16 -18)* when a girl who brought money into the house of her master through soothsaying followed Paul and the other apostles crying 'these men are servants of the most high God.' Paul was prompted by the Holy Spirit as to the origin of these cries and cast out the spirit from the girl so that they could continue with their ministry.

In the battle for the mind and soul of a person, it is very easy with the influences within our society to become affected by this spirit in some sort of way. God hates this because people can be drawn away from him in order to gain false knowledge from satanic sources, which can lead them into much greater problems. Knowledge is a powerful tool for the one who has acquired it. Satan will use the lure of knowledge to gain entry into the seekers life. It is only when Satan has a hold in their life that they find out that the knowledge they were promised is false.

Ouija boards also come into this category. What is often looked upon as a seemingly innocent game used at parties is in fact a tool used by Satan to gain access into the world for his demons and then they become active in the work of destroying God's creation. Ouija boards are extremely dangerous and are not to be taken lightly. I know of a group of school children who took part in a game of Ouija at a party. They did it as a piece of fun. The majority of the group were unaffected by this but one girl saw a face coming towards her from the board. After the game concluded, the face remained and attempted to control her actions. The demon masquerading as the face was seeking to dominate her and take her away from her Christian friends and the church she belonged to into a life filled with drug taking. Fortunately, after many years of struggle, the girl sought help from a deliverance minister and the demon was expelled from her life. The demon was acting as a spirit guide (see familiar spirits below).

- Familiar spirits

These spirits are usually involved in the supposed consultation with the dead (necromancy), spirit mediums, clairvoyance, yoga, spiritualists, psychic powers and prophecy, mind altering drugs and extra sensory perception to name just a few. Meditations on particular objects or false doctrines are used to open up the persons mind for demons to enter. Mind altering drugs, which tend to be illegal, are dangerous as they disorientate the user to the point of freely allowing the demons to enter.

The ability to contact the dead is often passed down through the generational line. Because of this, when a person who has this ability becomes a Christian, they can be demonically harassed because the familiar spirits within them still believe that they have a right over the person because of their ancestors involvement with the demon. They have no such right because they have become a new person in Christ. Blood ties (which are described fully later) need to be cut through deliverance so that the new Christian can walk free. Spirits within other members of their family may cause trouble for them and they also cause a breakdown in the relationships. Therefore family members may be aggressive towards the new Christian and may disown them. This is usually the demon working through them.

When the participant is 'contacting' a relative who has died for example, they are in contact with a familiar spirit masquerading as the dead relative. They then gain the persons trust and begin to work within the person's life and quite often become their 'spirit guide'. Spirit guides are demons that attempt to guide a person through life, often telling them the best course of action. This is the best course of action to fulfil the demons means and to entrap the person. Spirit guides often appear as a real person and can take on any form, even that of a close family member who is now deceased. They do this on order to fool the person that the relative is back in order to gain their trust. This only leads to the person's destruction.

- Spirits of jealousy

Jealousy is the oldest sin. It started before the earth was created. Lucifer was jealous of God so he rebelled and was consequently expelled from heaven. The root of this spirit are works of the flesh meaning the lust for power, wealth and status in society.

All through the Bible we find examples where men have become jealous, envious, have hated and caused strife. When this happens, you come away from God and his Holy Spirit and become under the control of the spirit of jealousy. This works by the spirit sowing the seed within the mind causing offending feelings and before you are aware, it is out of control.

- Lying spirits

It is important to realise that God never changes; he is the same today as he was in the past and as he will be in the future. God

ALWAYS speaks the truth. Satan on the other hand is an expert liar and will try his hardest to stop people believing God's truth.

This group of spirits are in control of such things as superstitions, lies and slander, gossip, false teachings, false prophecy and accusations. Cults and false religions are also in the control of, amongst others, lying spirits.

It is important that this spirit is dealt with in order for the person affected to come into a realisation that what they have heard is false. They then can listen, understand and accept the truth that God has to offer.

- Perverse spirits

This group of spirits attack the person's mind and lead to works and sins of the flesh. It can cause total disruption and the breakdown of many people's lives because of one situation. Many people get so involved with this spirit that they begin to think that their lifestyle is normal. Examples of this are homosexuality, child abuse, pornography and other sexual perversions. They try and get respectability for their way of life, but God never changes. These things were a perversion in the Bible and still are today.

- The spirit of pride

Proverbs 16 v 18 says *'pride goes before destruction and a haughty spirit before a fall'*. Pride has to be one of man's greatest downfalls. We are told in society to achieve everything that is possible for us and then we will make it. This is what the spirit of pride tells us.

Due to Adam's sin, it is felt that each one of us is born with a spirit of pride. The way our society dictates to us only helps to strengthen the spirit within us.

The Holy Spirit tells us to be humble before God and seek his guidance in everything that we do. We have to bind this spirit in each one of us before it destroys us.

- Spirit of heaviness

This is directly responsible for heaviness of the heart, depression, despair and hopelessness, insomnia, sorrow and grief, suicidal thoughts and feelings of rejection. It may be argued that this spirit is a direct cause of mental illness that is brought about by the demonic.

Many people suffer with these symptoms and go to medical professionals for help. This is good as much counselling is needed but deliverance is also needed. The sufferer needs to know God as comforter and needs to learn to praise God with all their heart. When these happen the spirit is bound and the symptoms will go. It is important for the sufferer to be careful of what medication is prescribed by the doctor, as many have mind altering properties and can leave them open to more demonic intervention.

- Spirit of whoredoms

This group of spirits are responsible for many things including unfaithfulness and adultery in relationships, prostitution, worldliness and idolatry.

Idolatry can take many forms, a sports team, television programme, a famous personality, money or a partner or family member. These become idols when the focus shifts from God to them. They are all forms of worldly god's that this spirit loves to promote. We have to spiritually tear down and destroy every idol in our lives and lift Jesus high.

- Spirits of infirmity

This group of spirits are responsible for many serious illnesses and bodily afflictions. This spirit attacks the flesh in a big way. It can cause arthritis, asthma and other allergies and diseases such as cancer. It can also lead to infertility. It has been identified that there are specific cancer spirits which bring about the disease on a persons body. Maybe this is the reason why many cancers are not cured. Human medication cannot cure what is a spiritual problem. Deliverance can take away these spirits. Then the body may recover.

- Deaf and dumb spirits

These spirits are the cause of the attacks on the flesh but also affect the mind in serious ways. It can cause such afflictions as epilepsy and seizures to many different degrees of mental illness. People can also feel suicidal when oppressed by this spirit.

The spirit focuses a lot on children and many can be harassed by this spirit without anyone realising until it has such a tight hold. By this time medical science begins to run out of solutions and the power of God is needed to overcome the spirit. Serious prayer and fasting may be needed to successfully overcome this spirit.

- Spirit of bondage

These spirits trap people into actions that they seem unable to shake off. This spirit is one of the contributing factors of habitual sin, where sinful behaviour becomes almost a routine part of life. Habitual sin is a major problem, as there seems to be no way of stopping it. You become very fearful and may come to fear death. These spirits also cause many addictions including addiction to alcohol, substance abuse and pornography. It may also include an addiction to violence, the use of bad language and general abusive behaviour.

- Spirit of fear

I believe that there is both positive and negative fear. The positive fear stops us from walking out in the road with a bus speeding towards us. The fear is generated by past events that have been learned and become a natural response - part of your natural defence mechanism. The negative fear is quite often a fear that something unknown could happen in a situation. It is this negative fear that Satan grabs hold of. From this comes nightmares, doubt, insecurity, fear of other people that you may come into contact with, anxiety, stress and death. The fear may lead to the development of phobias which involve the item that is perceived to be fearful.

Satan will use this fear any way he can to stop us being used in some way by God or to stop someone escaping his clutches. This is the spirit that forbids the victim to utter holy words and the holy name of Jesus.

- Seducing spirits

These spirits are those directly involved in false religions. False religions can be defined as those that are contrary to God such as religions of the Far East and many man made religions that eventually become forms of cults. Many people are turning to false religions to find spiritual enlightenment and help for their lives. They then get entrapped by cults that lead them to destruction. These spirits make the cults seem correct and attractive. Many spirits contrary to the Holy Spirit possess many if not all of the cult leaders. The main spirit is of deception which causes hypocritical lying and the seduction of vulnerable people with fragile souls. I referred earlier to the newspaper articles for spiritual assistance. Seducing spirits are also behind these adverts to ensure that they appear attractive, positive and correct. They help to entrap many thousands of people and ensure that the gospel of Jesus Christ is not sought or heard.

These spirits can also work through some forms of popular music to entice certain behaviour or it's listeners and then trap them into crime, deception, Satanism and death.

- The spirit of the Antichrist

This spirit denies the death of Jesus Christ and the atonement. It is directly against Christ and his teachings. It is a big deceiver and teacher of heresies.

This spirit is directly responsible for secular society and the turning away from God and the church. This spirit loves anything that is not of Christ and is in direct opposition to him. This spirit tries, quite often successfully to change people's world view from that of the biblical to another that does not involve a direct relationship with his creator God.

- Spirit of error

These spirits never work on their own. They usually work with spirits of divination, lying or Antichrist in order to bring about a spiritual blindness. They promote the work of Satan and try to ensure that those affected believe that the things of God are false. Those affected by these spirits can never see that what they are doing is wrong and not of God and consequently damaging their life. This spirit is at work in many areas of modern life but especially in the New Age movement where the member's error is that they believe that Satan is the good force and God is bad.

- Spirit of death

This is the final enemy that anyone will have to face. The death of the believer is the ultimate victory for Satan. This spirit is a destroyer and it's only focus is to bring around death. This spirit will attempt anything to kill it's host. It does not care about the person. Once it has completed it's task of murdering the host, it simply moves on to the next person that invites it in.

People affected by this often have more than one spirit of death within them. A common way for the spirit to accomplish it's mission is through bringing in disease spirits such as cancer or bringing about the persons suicide. These demons are real team players as they need others to help them work. At the end of the day though, they only look out for themselves.

Christ won the victory over death on the cross so in turn we now have the God given authority over the spirit of death. We have no need to fear this spirit.

There are two main ways for a demon to enter a person. Through the person's sin and through curses that have been put upon them through Occult practices. Once these acts have been committed, the demon can claim entry and a right to the person. Curses can be laid on the person themselves or it could have been laid on one of their ancestors (generational curse) which is then passed down the family line. All curses can be broken through the name of Jesus. Both sin and curse must be repented of in order to take away the right the demon has to the person's life. Generational curses must be repented in the same way, you must repent for the sins of your ancestors.

How Satan and his demons attack people in today's world.

Satan attacks Gods special creation in the subtlest of ways. We only have to look at society today and see how much people are turning away from God to search after spiritual things. This is exactly the same as took place in the Old Testament. If we look in the book of Exodus we shall see how the children of Israel became so disheartened with Moses and ultimately God that they began to seek to live their lives in a different way. Their lives began to turn away from God with alters being made to many pagan gods.

If we look around we can see how people are focussing their attention on other gods. The gods of materialism and secularism to name just two are used by Satan to drive a wedge between God and his people. People are searching for spirituality. They are once again realising that they need faith in something because the world is in such a turbulent state, the world economy is in serious trouble and the system of family life has broken down, for many irretrievably. They are starting to discover spiritual things once more. Unfortunately in many cases the spirituality that they are receiving is not from God. If we are going to win people back to God we first of all need to make God and his church attractive to the non believer. We need to continue picking up the pieces of our broken society but also find a way to stem the brokenness. In order to achieve this we need to understand the methods that Satan uses to lure the weak and vulnerable away from God.

Now more than ever in the history of our society has magic become so socially acceptable. Our Pagan society is doing a great job at recruiting the young in a way that they don't realise. Books on the Occult and spell books are quite openly available next to the Bibles in many of our bookshops. Tarot cards are given away free with magazines and you can also collect weekly magazines on witchcraft.

The Pagan festival of Halloween has become one of the biggest holidays of the year, with children dressing as witches, demons and ghosts as they go trick or treating. Halloween also has a disastrous spiritual implication as many demons 'come out to play' on this night and cause havoc. While in Dallas, Texas, the friend that I was travelling with was affected in this way on Halloween. A demon manifested on a flag pole to her and stated that it was going to cut her and go inside her. Of course, it did this and deliverance was needed to get rid of the Halloween demon. There are specific Halloween demons that only come out on this night.

Satanism is becoming 'cool' with a teenage population, although many of them do not know what real Satanism is because they just follow the crowd to fit in and become popular. The internet is a great source of information. Anybody can create a web page and get their ideals and voices heard all around the world. Satan is using this for his own means. Demonic led people are creating pages to entice those that are searching. The pornography industry has been given a new lease of life, members of the Occult have open forum sites which attract the naïve. If misguided individuals that are entrapped by demons begin to use the internet to it's full extent, it can become very dangerous indeed.

If we were to look at television, witchcraft and the Occult are the basis of many popular television programmes. As I write this, a programme glorifying the existence of demons is being shown in a prime time slot for all to see. While these are all good television they spark off a great interest. Once the interest is there, Satan sets to work encouraging people to take it one step further and just 'dabble' in magic because 'it won't do them any harm'. Or the user may perceive that it does not work because it is just on television. Unfortunately what the viewer does not know is that there is more truth in the television programme than they realise. Many of the writers and producers are demon influenced. Satan then wins the viewer over because he has little opposition and his victims become blind to anything else. Before they know it, they are in too deep and it takes over their lives and they begin to wonder why things are going so badly.

I have recently read the series of Harry Potter books. They are well written fantasy books about a group of friend's adventures at a school for witchcraft. As I read the books I could see a darker side to them that may not be totally obvious to the average reader. I saw within their pages such issues as demonic possession, psychic writing, fortune telling, charm and curse casting. Through reading these books children have been known to start an interest in witchcraft and causing problems for many as their interest has increased and become dangerous. I have also been made aware through the Holy Spirit that the reading of these books by children within our church services has had a negative effect and has put up strongholds against the moving of the Holy Spirit within the service. We have to be careful and use our own judgement over this. We have to look at both sides. They are a good compelling story but if the interest is allowed to spark it can be dangerous. They teach both sides of the coin. They illustrate the battle between good and evil and outline the dangers of the kingdom of darkness but the magical elements are shown to be very attractive. In many children, the interest does not develop and they just read the story believing that it is just fiction but there is a large proportion that takes it further and tries the magic and psychic acts out.

There are two sides to look at in regard to acting on what is read. On one side demonic activity is a very real possibility and something that we as Christians must acknowledge. On the other side they could just be making things up and wanting to believe something is happening. Either way, Satan will use it.

Take for example the story of a sixteen year old boy who was a huge Buffy the Vampire Slayer fan. He watched the show, read the books and bought the merchandise. He soon began to dabble in magic as one of the leading characters does. He bought some books of spells and tried them out. At first nothing happened. One night he had a dream and the dream seemed to loosely fit the events he saw on the news the following day. He tried some more spells and this time they worked. He continued to occasionally have his dreams that he now believed were psychic visions. At a friends party, they took part in a game of levitation because they thought that it would be fun to try, he was the only one of the group that successfully levitated.

Time passed and he began to suffer nightmares that seemed to get out of control and he found that he could not wake himself from them until it had finished. As these continued, he began to hear a voice as real as someone sitting next to him encouraging him to cut himself. At first he refuses but as the voice intensifies and becomes more and more angry he gives in. The voice now tells him that he is in control and begins to dictate his life.

The boy's sleeping patterns change and sleep becomes almost non existent. He becomes verbally violent towards his family and physically hurt some Christians at his school because they were talking about what they were going to do at church.

The pressure became so intense as the voice said that he was going to destroy him that he sought help from the school counsellor who in turn sent him to a doctor who said that it was just exam stress and sent him on his way.

Tragically, things became too much for him and he committed suicide leaving a note saying that 'he told me to do it and I have to obey him'.

This is the reality of Satan's attacks. Satan is intent on destroying God's special creation and will use the subtlest methods to achieve this. We as Christians need to be aware of this and be open to the Holy Spirit's leading to show us where demonic activity is taking over someone's life. We need to act in order to save the person. I know that in reality it is easier said than done but if it is God's will for us to be involved in this very important ministry, He will bring people to us. Reputation in this ministry field will be gained and God will draw more people to us. We just have to play our part and leave ourselves totally open to the Holy Spirit's leading.

- *Strongholds over churches and households*

The demonic hierarchy is very organised. There is a ruling spirit in control over whole regions and countries. These are often referred to as territorial spirits. Underneath them are other spirits that control churches, households and individuals. This means that even our safe churches can come under the control of Satan and his demons. This then can have an effect on the individuals within the church.

Some time ago I was given a vision of a dark cloud over a church that I attended. The oppressive cloud was very large and encompassed the whole building. Individuals, including the decision makers and elders of the church also had clouds attached to them and their faces were dark. A word of knowledge revealed that there was a percentage of the members that were involved in witchcraft and some were members of the Freemasons.

The actions of the individuals affected were unchristian. There was much internal fighting within the church, many people were leaving or being forced to leave for many unjust reasons. Illness and death were evident within the fellowship. The stronghold over the church needed to be broken, but many in the fellowship had been blinded to that fact. Christian people who were open to the working of the Holy Spirit were becoming isolated and felt that their efforts to change the situation were in vain.

In their blindness, prayer vigils were kept and they tried to make the church attractive for new people to come and worship and wondered why people didn't come and why established members began to leave.

Unless the stronghold was to be broken the church would fail to progress. The church became insular and because the leadership was strong but misguided, the foundations became rocky.

When through prayer the stronghold was destroyed, the Lord moved in and began to heal the broken people in the fellowship. God undertook a spiritual cleansing of the church. Within months of each other, those identified to be involved with the works of Satan died after a short illness leaving the rest of the church to grow. There are now new fulltime leaders and the church has grown considerably. There are now two churches in one. The first caters for the traditional British congregation; the second is an increasingly growing and vibrant church that is catering for the immigrant Czech community. It has become a useful tool for God within their community.

The same can be seen within households. One person's spiritual suffering could be the result of another persons act within the household that has caused a demonic strongman to be placed over the household to control it. This may result in a generational curse being laid on the family members or a family member being involved in a satanic influenced activity, quite often without them realising what is happening. This may be through visiting the wrong kind of internet sites or even inviting someone into the home who happens to lay a curse on it.

I once worked with a Nigerian Salvation Army Officer who told me that when he became a commissioned officer he began to see revival start in his ministry but his leaders did not like this so he was moved to another church which was in a very hard area. The town he was sent to was notorious for Voodoo and Witchcraft and the previous leaders did not make a stand and ended up defeated. Many turned away from their faith, others were killed, but my colleague felt God was telling him to stand against the forces of darkness and he led a united churches rally and saw over 4000 people turn to Jesus in one day. He was deemed to be a trouble maker and subsequently moved to England so that he was out of the way.

The demonic stronghold over Nigeria is so strong that it penetrates through the government and tribal leaders to all the fabric of society including the church. Satan hates the kingdom of God being revealed on earth so he will even attempt to influence the sets of power within the church in order to stop the advancement of God's kingdom. The same type of stronghold could be seen over the old Soviet Union. The territorial spirit was influencing the godless society, as it still is in China. We can now see that the spirit of God has broken through in Eastern Europe through the prayers of the Christian faithful in the west. The same is beginning to occur in China.

- *Spiritual Armour*

None of us are very good when faced with pressure and uncomfortable situations. You could be the greatest at keeping calm under pressure and know all the latest techniques for keeping control under immense pressure, but when it comes down to it, the pressure that can attack our spiritual lives at one time or another gets us all. We may be faced with subtle persecution from work colleagues and friends and could feel backed into a corner by a doctrinal question posed to us while we are off guard and designed in a way to trip us up and make us look foolish. We can be driven down many ways, often so discrete that you do not realise until it is disastrously late. It is often the case that the greatest and most ferocious type of attack can come from fellow Christians. In my experience, I have found that the non believers have been more open and tolerant to the true Christian way of life. I make a distinction between this and the religious show way of life that many believers get caught up in.

That is why we as Christians have been given spiritual armour to protect us when the attack is on.

> '...be strong in the Lord and in His mighty power. Put on the full armour of God so that you can take your stand against the devil's schemes. For our struggle is not against flesh and blood, but against the authorities, against the powers of this dark world and against the spiritual forces of evil in the heavenly realms. Therefore, put on the full armour of God, so that when the day of evil comes, you may be able to stand your ground. Stand firm then, with the belt of truth buckled round your waste, the breastplate of righteousness in place, and with your feet fitted with the readiness that comes from the gospel of peace....Take up the shield of faith which you can extinguish all the flaming arrows of the evil one. Take the helmet of salvation and the sword of the spirit, which is the word of God. And pray in the spirit on all occasions with all kinds of prayers and requests....be alert and keep praying.' (Ephesians 6)

Every time I read this, I think of Sunday School. How many times have we dressed up in cardboard armour to illustrate how God protects us against bad things? But as we get older and grow in faith it is very important that we take these things in hand.

In order to explain the ideas of the protection that God gives us to the first century Christians, the apostle Paul used military terminology which all citizens of that time would have known well. The ruling power of that time were the Romans and each soldier was fully armed and protected from head to foot before they were allowed to go into battle. The Roman armies were so successful because of how protected they were and how they worked as a team. It was the same for the Christians then and the same for Christians now. We need to be fully protected before we can engage in battle against the evil forces at work in this dark world.

Let us now take a look at each item of the armour in turn.

- The belt of truth.

    We need discernment to know the truth. To discern clearly it is important that we do not judge. We must keep the mind of Christ at all times acting and doing as he would. Only then will we hone our spiritual discernment. This discernment also comes through prayer and meditating on the word of God. Through this, God will help us discern what is right and wrong in a situation, what is demonic and what is of our own worldly creation. God will give spiritual wisdom.

- Breastplate of righteousness

This piece of armour protects our hearts and our love for God. This is an area that can be attacked heavily. Satan will try to deflect our love away from God to more material things. We need to be strong in our love for our heavenly father and believe in his love for us even when things are hard and it seems like he is far away and leaving us to our own devices. God is in total control. We need to keep our love strong.

- Shoes of the gospel of peace

    These help us to walk in the light of God. We need to keep on the right track with him to be used effectively.

- Shield of faith

    The shield is an important part of any military equipment. It is needed to deflect the onslaughts of the enemy. The 'fiery darts' of Satan can cut through anyone and cause devastating effects. The shield protects you from these arrows. The shield can be put into practice through the use of scripture to extinguish the fire sent towards you.

- Helmet of salvation

    The helmet of Salvation is needed to protect your mind from interception through evil thoughts that lead to sin. The helmet must be worn at all times and is strengthened through prayer.

- Sword of the spirit

    This is used to attack Satan through the word of God. In ministry, I have often seen the Bible used in a way similar to a sword that has caused a devastating effect on the demon being dealt with.

Why is it that Christians talk about the spiritual armour and maybe even put it on for a time but then it is taken off and they are left open to attack? The armour is taken off in the good times and then as soon as things turn bad they wonder why they are left in turmoil and under pressure. I think we are all guilty of this to some extent. Satan will take any opportunity to send one or more of his demons to attack the Christian while their guard is down.

Always keep your guard up, however you feel. Keep resisting evil and you will remain an active fighting force for God.

Practical tools given by God for ministry.

How is this armour used in the day to day reality of the fight for peoples' souls against Satan and his demons? Many practical tools have been given by God which along with the spiritual armour give us the full weaponry available to us not just in a ministry situation but in our every day walk with him. We shall look at these in no particular order.

1. Prayer (see also prayer and fasting)

    This is a vital tool given to us as without it and the practice of it nothing can happen. It is very important that this method of communication given to us is two way and that we do not allow our sins to interfere and disrupt this.

2. God given authority

   When we stand in front of Satan's forces in the name of Jesus, we have been given the authority by God to deal with the demons in the way that God has pre chosen for them to be dealt with. With this delegated authority, the same authority handed down to the apostles in Acts, and for every follower since, the demons must obey. The Bible says that at the name of Jesus every knee must bow *(Philippians 2 v 10)*.

   God has given spiritual authority to parents over their children, but when a daughter gets married, this authority is passed from the father to the new husband to exercise. This is important to note if ministering to a person who has issues to resolve in the past when the father had spiritual authority. It is hard to take out a demon if the father is a non believer. If the husband is a believer, these matters can be resolved as the authority has passed over to him. This is especially important to remember when dealing with such things as generational curses and dealing with cults where the parents are members.

3. The robe of Jesus

   This is an important ministry tool. It refers to the blood stained robe that Jesus wore on his journey to the cross. The robe of Jesus burns the demons if placed around the person being ministered to and takes away their strength as it is supernaturally soaked in the living blood of Jesus. In practical terms, the robe can be any cloth or towel that has been dedicated as the symbol of the robe by the deliverance minister through prayer.

4. The blood of Jesus

   This is the warm living blood of Jesus and it is the most powerful weapon in the armoury. Call on Jesus to cover the demon in the blood and they scream in pain.

   The blood of Jesus will never lose it's power because it is divine blood. It is living blood. Evil spirits know they are defeated when the Christian uses the blood properly as a weapon in spiritual warfare. The blood of Jesus speaks destruction on the enemies of God. It provides healing to the Christian's body and must be used as a method of protection.

5. The name of Jesus

   All who call on the name of Jesus will receive his help and guidance. Demons tremble at the name of Jesus and it is through his name that they are sent to their final death in the pit (Revelation 19 v 20).

   Always minister in the name of Jesus and the victory over the demon is assured. Minister under your own steam and you will be defeated.

6. The cross

   The most recognisable symbol of Christianity that there is. At the sight of the cross people of every faith and those confessing no faith at all know what it represents.

Satan and his demons tremble at the sight of the cross because they know that through this piece of wood and the sacrifice that hung on it they were eternally defeated.

In ministry the cross is a very powerful tool. Demons tremble at the sight of it and it harms them greatly when they touch it.

While being involved in ministry in the United States, a demon covered up a large wooden cross in the basement of the church as a sign of defiance. While ministry was being undertaken upstairs in the main chapel it became apparent that the demon being dealt with was under orders from a higher ranking demon to carry out the act. Before the demon was cast out, God's holy angels were used to carry the demon (still within the human body) out of the chapel, down the stairs to the room where the cross was located. Once there, the demon was made to uncover the cross, kneel at the foot of the cross and after a mighty struggle declare that 'Jesus is Lord'. The angels then moved the person's hands so that the demon touched the cross. As the demon shook it was evident that it was losing strength. The demon was then taken by the angels back into the chapel to be cast out.

7. God's holy angels

As we saw from the above example, God's holy angels are very useful and often vital in the ministry of deliverance and also in our every day lives.

I believe that it is very important to pray for God to send angels into a situation. Throughout the Bible angels are used to send messages (the birth of Jesus) and are used in the same way today to send information between man and God.

Angles are there for protection. They guard us when we are about God's work. They also carry requests to God and warrior angels fight in the spiritual realm on our behalf.

Good angels are ministers of light who intercede on our behalf before the throne of grace. This is why it is so important to allow angels to carry out their work. Through our delegated authority, the Christian can command angels to carry out specific tasks that are permitted by God to aid in a ministry situation. For example, to restrain the human body so that no physical harm occurs, sing praises to God (*Revelation 4 v 8*) which tortures demons as they cannot bear to listen. They can use their swords to smite the demon, stand between the demon and the ministers to provide protection and bring comfort to those being ministered to.

Some people ask, can you see angels? Quite often the answer to this question is no, you can only see the results of their actions. I have seen angels restrain people to stop the physical body being hurt, angels can lift people up and move them around. One such incident occurred when a ministry session was taking place in a hotel room in North London. The demon caused the person being ministered to run into the bathroom, the angels then bound the demon and slowly moved the person back to the chair that they were originally sitting in. On another occasion a demon caused a person to lock themselves inside a hotel room and hide under a table at the other side of the room to where the door was. The demon locked the door from the inside which included a door chain. After praying and instructing the angels in the name of Jesus, we stood back and watched as the angels opened the door revealing the demonised person under the table. The person was then moved by the angels back to a car, sat down to be transported back to the church where the ministry was taking place.

A very good friend of mine who is a deliverance minister tells a story of when he was ministering to a Satanist who was a high priest in the religion. This man had recently become a Christian and had begun the process of taking out the many hundreds of demons within him. Within the course of the ministry session, the demons became so strong that they forced the man to run from the church. Outside, my friend and his associates saw the man being picked up from the ground and being pinned to the side wall of the church by God's angels.

Sometimes God does allow us to see his angels as they interact in our lives. This can happen in many ways, Firstly God could open our spiritual eyes to see them. I remember after a personal prayer session where I seemed to be wrestling with evil forces, I prayed for an angel to protect me while I slept. Soon after, I saw an angel standing at the head of the couch I was laying on resting his hands on his large sword. I felt an inner calm and slept well. When I awoke the angel had gone.

Secondly, an angel may appear in a human form. When I was taking part in a mission on Latvia, shortly after the borders were opened, the team I was in were in a coastal area not far from the capital Riga and were the only English speakers for many miles. The mission was very intense and involved some serious spiritual warfare which risked our lives on many occasions. Very early one morning, the team went to the beach to pray and sing worship songs. The beach was deserted for miles except for our group. All of a sudden an elderly man appeared and asked in perfect English if he could sit with us for a while and listen to our songs. We agreed and he stayed for some time. He eventually got up and said that he must now get on with other work and God is truly pleased with what we were doing and that he will honour it. He then left as suddenly as he arrived down the beach and just seemed to disappear. God sent an angel in human form to encourage us through our hardships in the same way he has done throughout history and will continue to do until the end of time.

We can be assured that if asked in the name of Jesus, angels will come to our aid in order to carry out God's will through the requests of the minister. There should be no doubt to this. Just ask the demons themselves and they will tell you exactly what is happening. Angels are around us carrying out God's will even if we do not know it.

8. Prayer and Fasting (linked to prayer)

I have found in recent days that fasting is a very important spiritual discipline for warfare and for effective and direct action. Spiritual fasting enables you to focus much more on God and you are showing commitment to God by depriving your body of earthly substance. Fasting may not be the right option for every situation but while you are fasting and focusing more clearly on hearing God's voice the human antenna is more in tune with heaven. Pray if contemplating a fast as God will make it clear whether it is the right option.

There are many options to fasting and includes one day fasting to three days fasting taking only liquid, to a total fast which means that you abstain from food and liquids for the given time of the fast. This is often called a supernatural fast as it is the type of fast Jesus undertook in the desert during the temptations. This type of fast should not be attempted over a long period of time for health reasons. Fasting enables us to take ourselves to a greater spiritual level that is not accessible through normal prayer.

It is important to offer up prayers of praise and intercession. Praise allows you to get your mind focussed on God and at this point allows the Holy Spirit to start ministering to our own spirits. This then needs to be followed with prayers of intercession. When we start to intercede on behalf of a person or situation our prayers bridge the gap between man and God. This can be very important if the person wants ministry but is unable to pray for themselves due to demonic intervention. The minister must bridge the gap on their behalf.

Prayer takes many forms, but I feel it appropriate to draw your attention to just a few. The Bible says:

'Ask and it shall be given to you, seek and you shall
find, knock and the door will be opened to you.'
(Matthew 7 v 7)

These are three important stages in prayer. First of all you ask the Lord for answers and solutions, then as the situation develops and gets more urgent you may seek and pray harder, when you are knocking on heaven's door with your prayers the prayers are urgent. Many of our spiritual warfare prayers in deliverance situations take this form.

Prayers can be offensive and defensive. Defensive prayers are often in the form of asking for protection; whereas offensive prayers are used as a full assault on the enemy. All spiritual warfare prayers must be uttered with authority and urgency and through the name of Jesus.

All this said, prayer does not need to be complicated. Some of the most effective prayers are the simple prayers that are often uttered by children.

9. Holy water

    Another powerful tool. This is often used within the church for the provision of blessings at times of dedication, christening and baptism.

    It is powerful in the deliverance ministry and is used principally in the same way as the robe. Demons hate the blessing that it gives and burns them. The use of holy waters both sprinkling and baptism breaks down the demon's armour and makes them weak. Water that is dedicated through prayer by the minister is sprinkled on the oppressed person when appropriate in the ministry session. How much is used depends on the situation and how stubborn the demon proves to be.

    Holy water is also used for dissolving devices that have been placed in the body by demons through satanic cults. These include seeds and tracking devices as explained earlier.

10. The Bible

    The Bible, God's holy word is truly a sword of the spirit. God's word is sacred and must be respected. The demons respect and fear it. They fear hearing the words that it contains and fear holding it. Demons tremble when they hold the word of God.

The Bible is used as a sword in ministry. If lightly placed on the body, the demons are pierced by it. If placed on the head, all the demons armour and mind control mechanisms are destroyed.

After ministry, the person being ministered to often states that they feel like they have been stabbed where the Bible has been placed on the body.

We must always ensure that when ministering to the oppressed, we use the mind of Christ and minister in love. If you fail to do this, the ministry is worthless and not of God. Serious problems could occur and demons could take advantage and cause devastation.

Faith

Time after time, as I talk to people who are questioning the things of God I hear them say *'but that was then this is now, God doesn't do that today...Anyway the Bible was written so long ago, how do we know that it actually happened, surely there is a rational explanation for the miracles and everything that happened in the Bible.'* They question the Bible and try and come up with rational scientific answers and get stuck every time.

I recently heard a story of a young Canadian man who enjoyed his life. He went around doing the things that people enjoy. He drank socially with his friends and enjoyed the gang violence scene. Like most young men, he loved to cruise the streets in his car to attract the girls. One night he and his friend picked up two girls. He offered one of them a drink, she declined and said that she didn't drink. He accepted that and in many ways admired it. At the end of the evening he dropped the girl off because she had to lead her Sunday school class the next day at her local church and she said that he should come to the church sometime to find out what it was all about. He just dismissed the idea and went on his way.

As time passed he realised that he liked the girl but he was rejected by her because he was not a Christian. One day he reached the lowest of the low after he had been in a fight which involved hitting a man until he was close to death with a large cast iron object. Thankfully other gang members pulled him off just before he killed the man.

He woke up the next day with the realisation that his life was in a mess. He was successful in business but his drinking and gang life was dragging him under. He admits that he knew he was at rock bottom when he could get so close to taking a man's life and think nothing of it.

He then went to church and was shown the life changing power of God and was drawn to Jesus in a real and powerful way. He married the Sunday school teacher and felt God call him into a specific ministry. At first, he chose to ignore this calling and saw his life slowly collapse around him. While recovering from a serious illness, which took him close to death, God came and miraculously healed him. He changed his views and accepted God's calling. He and his wife then entered full time ministry.

What we can learn from this modern example and the examples given by the Apostle Paul is that we need to have faith to believe the things that we cannot always see. If we have the faith to believe in God, he will open our eyes to the things of God. It takes a real act of courage by the individual to put the faith into practice.

If we look at the story in the Bible where the disciples are in the fishing boat and Jesus is on the other side of the river, Peter displays his faith by getting out of the boat and walking on the water to Jesus.

As soon as he takes his eyes off Jesus he begins to sink, but Jesus draws Peter's attention back to him and he makes it across the water.

We as Christians need to have the faith displayed here, the faith to get out of our comfort zone, the faith to get out of our own boat, whatever that may be. When we do, God will help us to walk by this faith. There may be times when the things of the world distract us and we may begin to sink and before we realise, we are struggling. When we call out, God comes to our side and picks us up and helps us to walk by faith once more urging us on to reach him.

We must have the faith to see and believe in the spiritual aspects of Christianity. We must have the faith to believe those oppressed that come to us, many with horrific stories of abuse, illness and spiritual oppression. Most of all we must have the faith in Jesus and the tools that he has given each and every one of us to act in his name, minister in love and bring about the kingdom of God in people's lives.

PART 2
Dissociation

We live in a very complex time. Our lives are getting busier and busier. Jobs become more and more demanding, social lives become more hectic as the technological age shrinks the world and social networking becomes a much greater phenomenon through the medium of the internet. Society thrives to some extent on adrenaline and stress and we develop complex coping mechanisms in order to survive.

What happens when it all goes wrong? When life gets the better of us and our highly developed coping mechanisms let us down. What happens when we are threatened by a third party and our world comes crashing down around us? The traumas that life can throw at us can have a devastating effect.

Trauma

Psychologists have identified two types of trauma that can affect a person. Emotional and psychological trauma. These are often the cause or result of immensely stressful events that threaten the person's sense of personal security. There could often be a threat to the person's life or safety which can lead to the person feeling very vulnerable and overwhelmed. There is often psychological harm involved in the act of the trauma although the factors and events leading up to the trauma can involve greater psychological harm.

Emotional and psychological trauma is quite often likely to occur if the event leading to the trauma happened unexpectedly or repeatedly and the victim is unprepared for the event, for example incidents such as a street mugging or knife attack, sexual assault or rape. It may occur if someone was intentionally cruel to the victim. The events leading to the emotional and psychological trauma is especially distressing if it happened in childhood. The victim almost always feels powerless to prevent the events leading to the trauma and the guilt of this may cause more issues later in life that will need to be resolved. A prime example of this is a child being abused by a parent or guardian. Due to the relationship set up between them the adult claims power and control over the child. The child then feels powerless to stop the incidents. The threats of the adult are usually enough to silence the child.

Traumatic experiences

If emotional and psychological factors lead to trauma, we must identify what events can possibly lead to traumatic experiences. No-one is immune from events that cause traumatic experiences but there are some devastating effects. This is often quite prolific if the traumatic events occur at a young age in childhood.

Traumatic experiences can be caused by such events as:

- A significant fall or a painful sports injury.

- The worry and fear that can develop through the uncertainty of a surgical experience and the fear of entering a clinical environment. This is an occurrence that I deal with frequently in my every day working life in dental health regulation. The fear of people going to the dentist and entering that environment is often greater than the fear of the actual dental surgery. This is a great indicator of trauma and often stems back to childhood where the dentist was someone to fear or from a previous dental experience that may have gone wrong. This fear that often occurs in childhood is a real fear of the unknown that a parent or guardian cannot alleviate.

- The sudden death of a family member or close friend. It can also be a traumatic experience if the person was suffering from a long term illness.

- An auto accident. This incident does not need to include injury or death, although these are very traumatic, the shock of the event can also be a trigger to trauma.

- The breakdown of a significant relationship. This can include the breakdown of a marital relationship, the relationship between a parent and child or the relationship between a close group of friends.

- The disappointment and upset that can occur if a situation does not go as planned or does not go the way that you intended it to.

- A deeply humiliating experience that can leave you embarrassed and unable to face a particular group of people or situation.

- Although a joyful experience to be celebrated, childbirth can be very traumatic for both mother and the new born baby.

- The discovery of a life threatening or disabling condition.

As discussed earlier, childhood experiences can be a major cause of trauma which can cause devastating effects on the child for the rest of their lives if it is not dealt with swiftly and effectively. Unfortunately many childhood traumas can remain undetected because the child is unable to express what has happened to a responsible adult, or the child themselves do not realise what has happened and the gravity of the situation they were in. Childhood's traumatic experiences can include:

- An unstable or unsafe environment. This is evident in situations where the child has a home life where they are possibly neglected by their parents or guardians or moved from place to place due to the acts of their carers. They may also be moved from home to home while in the care of such organisations and governmental departments as Social Services and other children's homes.

- Not being shown any love by those who are caring for the child. This is also a form of neglect.

- The separation from a parent through their death, being lost and unable to find the parent in a public place or being taken into Social Services care.

- Serious illness

- Intrusive medical procedures. This could be through legal medical procedures that take place in a hospital which cause the child great concern or illegal medical procedures which may be undertaken by a carer or maybe as part of cult activities. This is also a major form of physical and possible sexual abuse.

- Sexual, physical or verbal abuse. In today's world many people are beginning to tell their story of how they were abused as children. Many scandals are now coming to light of how organisations have allowed their staff and members to carry out many types of abuse against children. This is even more terrifying if the abuser is the child's carer. We shall look at this issue in greater depth later.

- Domestic violence. It is staggering how many children are still suffering from violence in their own homes and are forced by the abuser to keep it quiet. So many of these children, and many adults that are suffering from acts of violence in their own home slip under the radar as people do not pick up the signs and the violence keeps on happening. Who is to know what happens within a house once the front door has been shut.

- Bullying by adults and their peers.

If both adults and children are suffering from significant traumatic experiences, how can we recognise the signs that a traumatic incident has occurred. It is very difficult to spot the signs as many have adjusted their natural coping mechanisms to accommodate the effects of these events, in an attempt to deny that the incident happened, and to cover up any knock on effects that it has caused.

A natural coping mechanism is a function that the body implements in order for a person to be able to withstand a particular experience. This function is developed over time and is based on previous experiences which allow the body to try and determine the outcome of the situation and to adjust behaviour accordingly. In the majority of situations, the older the person is, the greater this response would be. This though would not be true if it is a brand new experience. The body would learn from the experience and adjust behaviour accordingly if the situation arose again. To take a simple example, you are learning to ski. You have never stood on ski's before and have never been down a ski slope. Your body does not know what is going to happen. You stand on the ski's and immediately lose your balance and fall over. You get up and try to adjust yourself to remain upright. You fall again, get to your feet and once more fall down. Eventually you master your balance and remain upright. Your body has learned from the experience and has adapted. A natural coping mechanism has developed which will now kick in whenever you step foot on ski's.

Many of the symptoms which occur after an incident, occur within the person's psychological makeup. These symptoms can be difficult to hide as they occur in the subconscious mind, which can be hard to keep under control, and the sufferer is often not aware of them until a situation arises and they come to the surface of the conscious mind. These symptoms can include:

- Insomnia

- Nightmares

- Being startled easily

- A racing heartbeat, especially when faced with something connected to the incident or a situation that reminds them of it.

- Aches and pains

- Fatigue. This can be connected to the problem of insomnia.

- A difficulty concentrating on a task which can bring about an ability to relax.

- Edginess and agitation

- Muscle tension.

The emotional symptoms of a traumatic incident are generally easier for the sufferer to cover up and try to avoid as they occur in the conscious mind. Although the sufferer may be able to do this, over a substantial amount of time (this could amount to a number of years), the cork will eventually come out of their bottled up emotions. It is at this point that a caring person needs to be on hand so that they can share the emotions and allow the grief to come out and the healing to start. The outward emotional signs of a traumatic experience can include:

- Shock, denial or a sense of disbelief that the incident has occurred.

- Anger, irritability towards others and vast mood swings.

- A general feeling of sadness or hopelessness which can lead to one of the many forms of depression.

- General confusion as the sufferer may find it hard to concentrate on routine tasks.

- Anxiety and fear.

- Withdrawing into themselves and away from others.

- Feeling numb or disconnected from those around them. A sense of looking at the present situation they are in as a third party outsider or as if they are watching the current events unfold on television.

As discussed earlier, traumatic experiences can have devastating effects on children. Unlike adults, children do not have a vast amount of worldly knowledge and have not had a significant amount of life experiences to learn from and fall back on. Due to their age and inexperience, they have not developed their coping mechanisms as far as adults have. So when a potentially traumatic experience happens for the first time, because it is a brand new experience, it is doubly devastating. The coping mechanisms of some children can develop at a much greater rate especially if abused or find themselves in a situation where they become primary carer for a parent. This may cause them to lose their childhood and their childlike vulnerabilities. They then often appear older than their years. This is just an appearance that they have developed as part of their natural coping mechanism.

It can be debated that the most frequent cause of traumatic experience comes about through the abuse of power and control that an adult has over a child. This abuse of power can lead to sexual, physical and emotional abuse which, if repeated can lead to devastating emotional and psychological disturbances that can be almost impossible to get over.

The extent of violence against and the abuse of children are still unknown. Even though many are now brave enough to speak out against it, there are still many that have not found a voice and their situation remains unknown as they continue to suffer. Statistics from the National Society for the Protection of Cruelty to Children (NSPCC) state that in a study undertaken in 2000, there was a 69% return from a pool of 2869 18-24 year olds which stated that 21% of females and 11% of males that responded had suffered some form of child sexual abuse. (Source: NSPCC.co.uk). These are only representative of a sample of the population and a true count is difficult to undertake because of the unwillingness of some participants to face the issues that have been inflicted upon them, which is perfectly understandable.

The emotional and psychological scars that are generated through trauma become deeper and deeper as they grow into adulthood. As we shall see in the next section, the soul can reach a state where it is very difficult to recover, sometimes breaking into pieces.

It is important to note that severe trauma can have a devastating effect on anyone's life; it is thought in the scientific and medical worlds that it can be completely irreversible. This is especially poignant if the trauma occurs in childhood. Due to the fact that the child has not developed their own coping mechanisms, the soul can suffer in ways that are hard to comprehend. The soul can cause the person to dissociate from people and everyday life as a form of enforced coping mechanism. As we shall discuss later, as Christians we believe that Dissociation is a gift from God to enable the sufferer of the trauma to cope with everyday life. We shall look at the rarely talked of, but surprisingly common phenomenon of Dissociative Identity Disorder (DID) and how God has given this to the trauma sufferer to help them along their journey in life. We shall also have a look at the many other forms of dissociative behaviour, how this plays out in the spiritual realm and how it affects the sufferer.

Firstly we must identify the basis of what is known in the medical profession as Dissociation by looking at the scientific viewpoint of what Dissociation is.

Dissociation – A Medical Analysis

The internet encyclopaedia 'Wikipedia' states that Dissociation is *'an unexpected partial or complete disruption of the normal integration of a person's conscious or psychological functioning that can not be easily explained by the person'*. In lay mans terms this means that Dissociation is when the person's mind or soul reacts to the trauma that it has suffered. This then causes an alteration in the way the sufferer consciously carries out their life. The psychological effects described earlier occur but the sufferer does not know or realise that it is happening. It is thought that Dissociation is a psychological defence mechanism against extreme stress or trauma.

Dissociation (which is a collective term for a number of disorders) is quite often regarded as a normal response to trauma as it allows the mind to distance itself from experiences that are too much for the psyche to process at the time of the event. It is thought to be a mental process that severs a connection to a person's thoughts, memory, feelings, actions or sense of identity. As Loan A Turkus M.D (www.Dissociation.co.uk) puts it, *'Dissociation is the disconnection from full awareness of self, time and/or external circumstances. It is a complex neuropsychological process.'*

Dissociation is a naturally occurring defence against childhood trauma and it is thought that children dissociate more frequently than adults. If a child is suffering from extreme abuse, it can often be seen that the child withdraws within themselves and psychologically flees from the experience that they are suffering from. This is the development by the child of a dissociative defence mechanism and if this continues into adulthood, full dissociative disorders can develop. Some of these dissociative disorders may develop in childhood depending on the frequency or the intensity of the trauma, but may not be evident until adult life.

Through many years of scientific discovery, five dissociative disorders have been identified. Some more serious than others, but all develop as a result of serious persistent traumatic experiences often occurring in childhood.

1. Dissociative Amnesia – This is the situation where the sufferer is unable to recall important personal information and information regarding specific events. It could in some respects be compared to someone going to a party, consuming a high level of alcohol so that they have no recall the next day of any of the events that took place.

2. Dissociative Fugue – This is where the sufferer finds themselves in a place with no memory of getting there and sometimes with no knowledge of who they are. It may be true to say that if a person carries out a particular act of violence

and kills or injures someone, they may mentally block out the event so when questioned by the authorities at a later date, they have no recollection of what happened and believe they are innocent. This could be a form of Dissociative Fugue.

3. Depersonalisation Disorder – This was briefly discussed in the section on the symptoms of trauma. It is where there is a feeling by the sufferer of being detached from themselves, personal feelings or situations. They continue to function having awareness of the situations and continue to live believing that it happened to someone else. It could also be a form of denial.

4. Dissociative Identity Disorder (DID) – This disorder was previously known as Multiple Personality Disorder and is the main focal subject of our study of Dissociation. It is where there is an existence of two or more separate identities within a core person. Each personality being able to take control of the core.

5. Dissociative Disorder Not Otherwise Specified (DDNOS) – This is the label that is put on any dissociative disorder that has not yet been identified. If someone has DID, this label is usually used until a full diagnosis has been given. You must remember though that DID is a disorder in it's own right.

There are five main symptoms that have been identified that generally cover the different dissociative disorders. These are:

- Amnesia. This is especially prevalent towards the events of the trauma or things that remind the sufferer of or are connected to the traumatic incident.

- Depersonalisation. This is where the sufferer feels like they are looking at themselves from the outside, as if looking at the events as a third party observer or on television. The sufferer may also have detached emotions, feeling glossed over, in a trance or they may feel like a robot.

- Derealisation. This is the feeling that the environment is not real or is completely alien to them. This could include such points as experiencing familiar people as strangers. The sufferer may feel that they are looking at everything through a fog.

- Identity confusion. This is the feeling of being confused about who you are. This could include confusion about sexual identity.

- Identity alteration. This is a shift in identity. It can include different names and behaviours. This is most common in DID.

It is important to note that dissociative disorders are much more common than people realise. Dissociative disorders are often not discussed as there is little awareness of them. Therefore many people who are suffering from dissociative disorders remain undiagnosed and unable to receive the best help that they can. This can be the cause of much concern, anxiety and frustration for those suffering. The latest figures state that 1% of the population of the United Kingdom suffer from DID and 10 % have a dissociative disorder of some kind. The figures also state that 25% of the population of the United Kingdom have experienced a dissociative episode of some kind. As there is little awareness and acceptance of dissociative disorders within the medical profession, it can be presumed that these figures are in fact much higher than what is recorded.

It has been found that people that suffer from DID often do not appear to have any mental health problems although mental health issues can be present alongside. The broken personalities are very difficult to spot as they have learned to hide themselves so that the core personality can lead as normal a life as they can. The broken identities usually include a child and a personality of the opposite gender as well as the core personality. If you read scientific information on DID it leads the reader to believe that it is only possible to have those three personalities where in fact a sufferer may have many broken parts. Some cases I know have hundreds of broken parts. The broken personalities are collectively called 'alters' although they will take their own name to be individually identified by. It is known that more women than men are diagnosed with DID.

The medical profession and psychiatry in particular view DID as a mental illness and try and cure the illness with a concoction of drugs. The only thing that this achieves is to distress the alters. It does not make them go away. A psychologist who is counselling a friend who is suffering from this disorder, amongst other mental health issues has stated that drugs do not work. The mental health profession cannot cure this disorder and he is fascinated to learn more from the alters.

Things of the spirit cannot be cured with medication. Demons will not leave with medication (in fact they use it to meet their ends), likewise alters, which are a spiritual coping mechanism cannot be taken away with medication. They can suffer the same side effects as the core person but they cannot go. It is known for alters to have different side effects to the core person causing more distress to the whole person. The core person may feel sleepy due to the side effect of a drug but an alter may feel nauseous or may have hallucinations which will in turn have an impact on the core personality.

The mental health profession can identify what Dissociation is and can attempt to cure it. They will have little success as they are missing the most vital element in the healing process for DID sufferers; God. The Christian holds the key to the healing of DID. If only more understood. It is often found that those with spiritual gifts of healing and deliverance are able to successfully help these people once they have been made aware. Many people who are severely demonised are also suffering from DID due to the trauma that leads to the demonization. These personalities have to be identified and welcomed within the ministry setting to bring about full deliverance and wholeness.

We now need to put DID into perspective in order to help those who are suffering. It is part of the Christians commission to cast out demons and to heal the suffering, including those with many parts.

Dissociative Identity Disorder – The Christian Perspective

It is important to acknowledge the research carried out by medical science into DID. Much research has been carried out into how it occurs and what the implications are for the sufferer. Medical science can only go so far with its study of DID because it is missing a vital aspect out, that being God. Hence when looking at it from a purely scientific viewpoint, there still lies a large amount of mystery and many questions remain unanswered. They cannot correctly label it as a mental illness because it cannot be treated the same way through the application of drugs and cognitive therapy. Although DID has many medical implications, it is not a scientific phenomenon and can not be correctly understood in the medical science realm. It is in fact a spiritual occurrence. This may be the reason why many in the psychiatric profession still do not believe that it occurs. Science puts the phenomenon down to a chemical response to severe trauma and they cannot comprehend that God is in control of the situation and is enabling it to happen.

But why does God enable this to happen? We can agree with the scientists that DID is a coping mechanism and a response to trauma as are the many other forms of dissociative response. God allows this to occur so that the sufferer is able to carry on with life until the time arises for the implications of the trauma to be faced and healing to occur.

Dissociation is a gift from God to the sufferer of the trauma. God defragments the soul nature and creates personalities to hold on to the trauma but to also help and guide the sufferer.

To understand this further, it is important to look at what the Bible says about what makes up God's special creation.

- *The make up of human beings*

The first step in looking at Dissociation with a view to understand God's place in it is by looking at what the Bible says about how human beings are made.

God created each one of us in the image of himself with a body, soul and spirit *(Genesis 1 v 27)*. We were created as one entity, but with three distinct parts, which is how we are supposed to remain until we meet Jesus at the end of our lives. Unfortunately not all of us remain in that state as tragedy and trauma can occur in our lives which can literally tear us apart. *(Psalm 7 v1 - 2, Psalm 69 v 20)* We should desire to be one whole person in the image of God at all times.

The soul that each one of us was born with is an incredibly powerful thing. It is close to the centre of our being and it creates our emotions and consciously helps us communicate with God through our spirit. Although the soul nature is a very powerful thing it is also very fragile and can break (or fragment) very easily when severe trauma occurs.

The sufferer literally has a 'broken heart' and the physical and emotional pain from this is enormous (*Psalm 7 v 1-2, Psalm 69 v 20*).

Each one of us is born with a spirit linked directly to God. Unfortunately through man's sin, this link is broken at birth and lies dormant until a time of spiritual awakening when belief in God is sought and found and the two way communication is opened and developed once more. This is why it is so important for Christian parents to bring their children up in the faith and teach them the things of God so that they can come back into a relationship with him.

We must remember that God knows everything about us because he made us (*Psalm 139*). He knows how life affects us, and he knows better that we could comprehend how the traumas we face affect us internally. Thankfully God has created a mechanism for us to cope and carry on living. He has developed a way for us to escape the extreme evil that we may face, by defragmenting the soul nature (*Psalm 124 v 6-8*).

The defragmentation that occurs is similar to that of a computer hard drive. When you want to sort out your files in order for your computer to run faster, you press the defragment button and your computer groups all the files that are linked together and places them in compartments so that the free space is left all together. The computer forgets about the bad segments that have been put together until the user purposefully looks for them in order to deal with them and clean them out.

How does Dissociative Identity Disorder Occur?

As previously mentioned, we have been created with three distinct parts:
- The Body – This is the outward appearance. It allows us to interact in the physical environment and enjoy life on earth.

- The Soul – (or soul nature). This is our heart. The soul enables us to experience emotions and often directs the way we react to specific situations.

- The Spirit – This is our inner core, placed in there by God for communion with him. Although it can be harmed by our actions, it cannot be penetrated or changed in any way. Nor can demons occupy this part of our body.

Each section is a vital part of the human makeup and interacts with each other in an intricate way. If something goes wrong in our lives, then this system is rocked and severe consequences could occur.

If a person is abused or suffers any sort of physical or emotional trauma, the soul can be affected. If the soul was to remain in one piece, the sufferer may become so overwhelmed by the situation that they may not be able to cope anymore. This may cause them to become physically or mentally ill and in extreme cases it may even be the cause of their death. God loves and cares for each one of us. Although he cannot prevent anyone getting hurt through the things of life, he does not want to see us suffer unnecessarily *(Psalm 147 v 3)*.

When the trauma gets too intense for the sufferer, the soul can crack and break off into smaller pieces. God uses this to help in our suffering. He allows a new personality (commonly called alters) to form. These alters take on their own identity and personality traits. They also absorb all of the fear and hurt caused by the trauma so that the main personality (the core) can cope and continue living. The alter will hold all of the hurt and pain until the core is ready to face it and be healed. The alter quite often holds the intricate details of the events leading to its formation so that the bulk of the memory of the incident is wiped from the core's memory. The core can be unaware of the alters existence for many years until the time comes for it to be made known.

To make this very complex subject a little clearer, the following diagrams have been designed to illustrate how DID comes into being.

Diagram 1 – The Whole

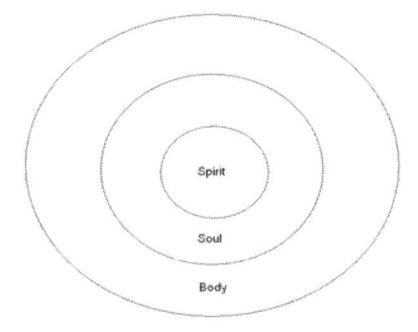

```
        Spirit
        Soul
        Body
```

This diagram shows how God intends us to be. The whole person with the spirit, soul and body complete. The spirit remains at the centre of the person, it is surrounded and protected by the soul which is in turn protected by the body. Nothing can penetrate the spirit however hard a demon may try. It is an enclosed area only accessible to God for vital two way communication with his special creation. The spirit will always remain intact however broken the soul and the body may become throughout life.

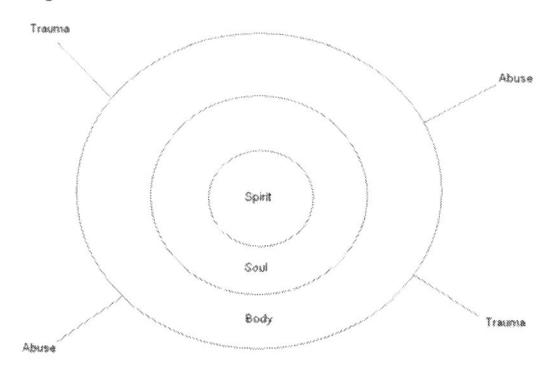

Diagram 2 – Affect of abuse and trauma

When abuse and persistent trauma occur, it has an affect on the body which is a person's first line of defence. It is often the body that is attacked through the events that lead to the trauma. The body is thick and can take a lot of pressure but severe abuse and trauma can get past the body's defences and penetrate into the soul nature which can cause metal scarring. If the trauma is severe enough, the soul can fragment and Dissociation can occur.

Diagram 3 – Fragmented Soul (Dissociation)

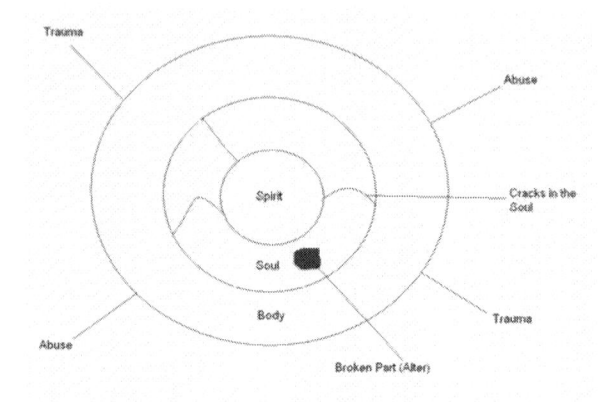

This diagram shows what could happen to the soul when extreme trauma occurs. The soul of the core person cannot cope with the trauma so it cracks and parts can break away. It is like a trauma being a cricket ball and the soul being a window. When the ball (trauma) hits the window (soul) the impact of this makes the glass shatter. These broken parts form the new alter personality which absorbs all of the information and feelings associated with the trauma. A person can develop more than one alter. This will be looked at in detail later. By this stage Dissociation has occurred.

As we have established how DID forms, now we must look in greater detail as to why DID forms.

Why does Dissociative Identity Disorder Occur?

Many of us live happy fruitful lives. We find ourselves well protected against the things that life throws at us. We have developed our in built coping mechanisms and have a tip top defence mechanism, which is constantly assessing the situation and adapting to it. We have been able to develop this over a number of years since we were children and we now know which situations to avoid.

Children on the other hand do not have this experience. As discussed earlier, every situation is new. When faced with a new situation they are unaware of the consequences and are unable to effectively handle what is thrown at them.

One of the major causes of fragmentation of the soul is sexual and physical abuse that is suffered as a child. The result of these acts on children especially if they are constantly subjected to them, and if carried out by people that they trust like parents or guardians can be emotionally overwhelming. Their souls are so fragile that they can break easily under the pressure. Unlike adults, children cannot physically run away from the source of the trauma, but they can internally run from the trauma and withdraw to a safer place which God has provided for them.

Alters are formed to allow this withdrawal to the 'safe place'. If a child is being routinely sexually abused, when the abuse starts, the alter that has formed because of that particular act of abuse comes to full consciousness to allow the core personality to withdraw and remain safe from harm.

Dissociation and in particular DID is God's gift to those suffering severe trauma which allows them to continue living and coping despite the ongoing abuse. He blesses the little children suffering abuse with this gift because he loves each and every one of them dearly and does not want them to suffer in any way.

Types of dissociative personality (Alters)

We shall look at some practical examples of the types of Alters in the next section but for now we shall discuss the types of Alters that are known to exist in more general terms. We need to identify what they are and how they could potentially have come into being. Four types of Alters have currently been identified.

- First generation

These alters are formed as a direct response to trauma. They are formed through the fragmented parts of the soul nature. One fragment of the core part of the soul creates one alter.

First generation Alters are unique to the DID sufferer. They are God's direct creation for the sufferer to enable them to cope and carry on with life.

- Ancestral personality

DID sufferers can sometimes find that they are aware of a personality that differs from all of the others. This is quite often because a dissociative personality dwells within them from another member of their family line.

As we are aware physical illnesses and ailments can be transmitted down the family line as curse and sin, as identified in section one. In the same way parts of the soul can be transmitted to another member of the blood line. This is usually caused through demonic power. The

Bible states that at the time of death broken parts of the soul can be disputed between Satan and the angels of God if a spiritual right has been given to the part. As we shall see later some alters are under the power of demons and they claim spiritual rights to them. Due to this dispute, the demons can implant the alter into another family member to meet their own ends. The sufferer will then find that they have knowledge of events that were before their lifetime. It is quite often an ancient memory but it has been known on very rare occasions for the part to be transmitted into a direct sibling.

This of course is used to God's advantage as the ancestral part has experience and knowledge which can be used to help the existing sufferer.

This will only occur if God permits it to happen for the greater good of the sufferer.

- Shared Alters

When alters are made they can be shared by two or more people. For example if two siblings are abused at the same time and both dissociate, because they have both suffered exactly the same trauma the same alter can form and be shared by both.

- Brothers, sisters and twins

It is also possible for brothers and sisters and twin personalities to be formed.

Twin alters are formed if the memory and emotions of the trauma are too great for one alter to hold. A second alter will form at the same time to share the pain.

Brothers and sisters come about in a similar way. One alter may be formed to deal with a trauma and then some time later, if a second trauma is experienced which is associated with the first, another alter will form and will have a direct relationship with the first alter. This will cause them to be siblings.

- *Cults and Dissociation*

Cults have been known to induce DID within a person in order to implant demons within the core. This is done so that the cult can keep control of the person throughout their lives. These alters are often described as bad alters.

- *Good and Bad Alters*

This is an area that can be misunderstood. The question is often posed that if Alters are a gift from God to help the sufferer of a trauma, how can there be bad Alters? This is an interesting point. It is true that Alters are given by God to help but demons can manipulate alters and influence them to do bad things through demonization and demonic harassment in the same way as they affect the core personality. This then could cause some alters to turn bad.

- *Names for alters*

Each dissociative personality that is made has it's own name for which they often choose themselves. They also develop their own distinct character traits. They know exactly what they like and what makes them happy. This can vary widely from the core's likes and dislikes. The age of the personality is derived from the age of the core personality at the time of the formation.

- *The Secrets of the Alters*

Alters exist as a defence mechanism but they also hold a wealth of information and spiritual insight which takes them to a different level of existence to what the scientists believe. Scientists may agree that the alters hold vital information regarding the trauma which is key to recovery, but will not accept the many other secrets that they hold.

When the alter is formed through trauma, all of the minute details associated with the event are siphoned into the alter, so that although the core personality may remember the event taking place, they will not remember the exact details which made the event so traumatic that it caused the alter to form. Most of the fear, hurt and emotional distress is also locked up inside the alter. Due to this, two things may happen with the core personality. Firstly, total amnesia may occur as the alter has taken onto itself all memory and feelings. Secondly, there may be a partial recollection of the events and emotional feelings caused, although the bulk and more serious thoughts and feelings are locked up inside the alter. The alter will hold all of this information until the events re occur causing previously stored information to be used by the alter to help the core through current events, or it will be released within a ministry session in order to bring about God's total healing.

It is important to remember that the alters communicate with the core even though the core may not be aware of the situation. This could be perceived by some as a form of schizophrenia and sufferers are often diagnosed as having this condition in the absence of a belief in DID. The alters will gently encourage the core through specific situations that they have expert knowledge of and also encourage the core generally through life. Once the core has established who the alters are they can build a relationship and hopefully become friends, although this is not always the case, so that they can work together for healing. It is known for alters to not get on with the core and try to take over as the dominant personality. Alters may not get on with each other through personality clashes which can lead to fights.

Alters can also bring great spiritual insight to all they know. We must remember that they are spiritual beings given by God. They have complete awareness and knowledge of the things of God, often putting Christians' knowledge of the Holy Scriptures to shame. Their eyes are completely open to the spiritual realm. They see both angels and demons and have great discernment.

Alters either see the spiritual light or they live in darkness, often being harassed by demons. Those who live in darkness can be shown the light by Gods Holy Angels and can be brought into the light and into a relationship with Jesus, the same as anyone can. Those alters who live in the light are known to have direct contact with Jesus and communicate with him. Jesus gives help to the alters but much of the information he gives is not disclosed.

If under attack the alters can retreat to a spiritual safe place. This spiritual place is described as a garden where all the little child alters can play. In the garden is a house where Jesus lives. Through the garden flows a river where when the water is drunk, healing takes place. The alters also talk of another garden in which they are not allowed to enter. It is stated that this garden is where all the people that have died go. They also state that the people who dwell in the garden enter the house where Jesus lives and do not come out. Jesus states in the Bible that in His fathers house there are many rooms and that he was going to prepare a place for each and every one of us *(John 14 v 2)*.

Demons and Dissociation

As we learned in section one, Satan and his demons will use any opportunity and areas of weakness to gain entry into a person's soul. The main entry for a demon is through sin and curse. When a persons mind is altered in any way, the defences come down and you can make yourself vulnerable to demons entering. This can happen through mind altering drugs or through acts of sin which could result in trauma. Unfortunately many who go through the trauma have some sort of level of acceptance of the act deep in the subconscious mind which can allow demons to enter. If, through the trauma an alter is formed, the demons may enter the alter rather than the core personality leaving the alter in a state of demonization.

Further parallels can be drawn in the demons that enter the alter are often related to the trauma. For example demons responsible for immoral sexual acts will enter through this type of abuse and demons of fear may come in through the trauma of persistent bullying. As with the demonization of the core personality, the demons will work hard to stop an alter from carrying out it's God given task. Not all alters become demonised but those who are live in the darkness and do not know Jesus because they are under the control of Satan.

Demons may choose to lock up alters in a remote area so that the core does not become aware of their existence. A strong demon will be in possession of the key and when being delivered it is important for the angels to locate the demon with the key and to unlock the alter before a healing ministry to the alter can begin. While the alter is locked up and under the control of demons, it is quite often the case that the alter will be subject to tremendous torture which adds to the trauma that it is already holding on to. This causes further difficulties to both the alter and the core. As we will see in greater detail later, a young baby alter (Ark) was sexually abused by demons for nearly twenty years before he was unlocked by an angel, received healing and was united with the core personality.

Alters act independently of the core personality so they may have demons that the core does not know about. If the core personality accepts deliverance ministry, the ministry may be hindered by an unknown personality that has demons. These demons will also need to be taken out before full deliverance is achieved for the core. If this is not discovered, it may be the case that the core personality and the minister believes that full deliverance has been achieved. However, because of a hidden demon within an unknown alter further problems could develop because Satan still has a foothold in the life of that person and can still bring in demons to strengthen his position. This will result in further deliverance being needed. You must treat each alter individually as they are there in their own right. Each alter must be delivered separately.

During the course of deliverance ministry, when calling up the next demon to be dealt with, it may in fact be an alter that comes to full consciousness. In this case you must identify using the spiritual test of asking whether they are human or spirit. If identified as human they are most likely an alter. You must then chat with the alter to establish who they are and the reasons why they are there. They also may know the existence of other unknown alters. You must also establish if they are living in the light and know Jesus or if they only see darkness which symbolises the presence of demonic interference. Alters can be very useful in deliverance ministry as they know exactly what is going on within the core person and most want the core to be healed so will share the inside knowledge in order to help.

In conclusion, God wants us to be of one mind, healed to worship and serve Him. For some, this requires a long spiritual battle against the forces of evil and further healing of alters. We must always remember throughout the process as either the minister or one receiving healing that Christ overcame all the forces of evil on the cross and through his resurrection we can win the battle for freedom. With this thought we can have peace.

> *"I have told you these things, so that in me you may have peace. In this world you will have trouble. But take heart! I have overcome the world."* (John 16 v 33)

**Part 3
Nataley's story**

I was born to Andrew and Louise Rogers on the 5th May 1987, in Ashford hospital. I was my fathers first child, as my mother had already had 2 children before me from another marriage, and he was delighted to welcome his first child into the family.

My father was an only child. His mother and father had not wanted other children so he grew up in Acton town with just his parents for company. He had a happy childhood, making lots of friends at school and enjoying all sorts of sport activities. He grew up to become a science teacher, working with senior school children. This is how he met my mother, who was the school nurse at the local school where my father was teaching.

My mother was a shy and unhappy lady, married to another man in a relationship that was mentally and physically abusive. She was leaving him, with the toughest decision of all, to leave her 2 young children. My father came along at just the right time. He was handsome, with a full head of dark hair and dark eyes. He made her feel happy and she laughed a lot in his company. He made her feel special and treated her gently and with the respect she deserved. After all, she was a beautiful lady, with a heart of generosity and love to offer. Her hair was golden brown and she had the biggest brown eyes he had ever seen. He particularly loved the way her face lit up when she smiled and the cheeky dimple by the corner of her mouth.

So the decision was made, she was to leave her family and move in with Andrew, eventually to become married to him.

Andrew was desperate to have a family of his own but my mother already had 2 children and had had the operation to cut off the fallopian tubes so she was unable to conceive again. However, during this time, a new procedure had been discovered, where women could have this operation reversed in order to conceive again. It was not 100% guaranteed to be successful but Louise and Andrew decided to find out more and go ahead with the operation. Just 6 months after the operation, my mother received the good news that she was now pregnant with me. My mother and father were overjoyed and decided to allow the professor that discovered and performed the operation to continue to monitor the pregnancy and be there for the birth of the child.

So, I arrived weighing 6lbs 7ozs and all was well. A year went by and my mother discovered she was yet again pregnant, having her fourth child. At 19mths old, I was given a beautiful baby sister called Susan. Our family was now complete.

My mother, who was a nurse in the local hospital at the time, decided to spend more time at home with her two youngest children whilst my father went out to work as a full time science teacher. However, this proved to be difficult as finances were tight, so it was then that the decision was made for her to return to work full time. This was fine by us children as it was decided that one of my mother's friends, who also had 3 young children, would look after us during the day until my father was home from work. Little did we know what the consequences would be of this arrangement.

Doris was a tall lady and very slim. She would wear leggings with two baggy t-shirts and a bright red jacket that had no sleeves. She wore very thick glasses and her eyes looked tiny under them. Her hair was greasy and black and always tied back in a long pony tail that reached her bottom. She was a very generous lady, always smiling and giving us sweets and biscuits when we went over there to play. She used to give us a babies bottle to drink out of and a chocolate bar, before letting us watch whatever we liked on the television.

She was married to Dave, although we never saw much of him. I don't think they got on very well as he was always out working and when he arrived home in the evenings they would argue and the children would be sent upstairs to play in the bedrooms.

However, I liked Dave. He was tall and gentle and when he was around he would play games with us and let us stay in the garden until it got dark. I remember one year, he did the most amazing firework display for us all. I was scared of the loud bangs but was allowed to watch from indoors and have a sparkler to hold. It was at times like this that I loved being at their house.

Doris had 3 children, Sarah who was the same age as me and twin boys who were a year younger. We all got on really well and played together every day. Sarah and I used to play mummies and daddies and we loved putting on Doris's lipstick and makeup. She never told us off for this and she seemed to enjoy watching us dress in her clothes and prance around the house with a face full of thick makeup. These days were great fun and I loved to stay the night with my little sister and have sleepover parties where we would play and dance to music all night.

However, these days were not to go on forever and things began to take a turn for the worse.

When I turned 3 yrs old, I would stay at Doris's house for one night a week with Susan. We would be allowed to watch cartoons on the television before bed and Doris would sit and watch them with us whilst getting the boys into their pyjamas.

One night, I can remember Doris entering the room, with no top on. We all laughed as she ran round the house, her breasts on full view for us all to see. As young children, we found this funny and clapped as she danced around us, semi naked. Following this night, she would continually walk around the house with no top on and eventually she decided to wear no clothes at all. I remember sitting next to her on the sofa watching my favourite cartoon, whilst she stroked and brushed my hair, totally naked. We would then be given a bottle of milk to take to bed and she would lie next to us until we fell asleep. This didn't seem to bother me as I was used to my mother laying next to me in my bed at home until I fell asleep.

One night she asked my little sister and I to sleep in her room as she said there was no longer room in Sarahs bedroom for the three of us. I lay in bed next to her and could feel her warm naked body against mine. This was the start of things to come.

I lay in bed, with my little sister one side and Doris the other. She breathes heavy and rubs her hands up and down her body.

'You must be hot. Take these off' she says, referring to our little mermaid pyjamas.
She helps us to undress and we lay back down, all three off us totally naked apart from our knickers, and we cuddle all night. This becomes part of our nightime routine from now on. We are 'hot' so we take our pyjamas off and sleep naked next to our abuser.

Whilst asleep, Charlie (an alter) comes alive. He is only three yrs old and already knows what is right and wrong. He lays in my place and I watch him toss and turn as the nightmares follow. Doris takes Charlie's hand and leads him to the boys room, where they are sleeping soundly. Pulling back the duvet covers, she reveals their tiny little bodies all snuggled up and totally vulnerable. She shows Charlie what to do and I watch as he pulls down their pyjama bottoms and touches between their legs. It feels warm and soft and Charlie begins to cry. He knows it is wrong. Doris is breathing heavy again and I run back to bed, sobbing in Charlie's arms.

Charlie becomes my saviour, my new best friend. He comforts me and holds my hand when we go into the boys room on those horrible nights. I begin to dread the sleepover parties, the cartoons on the television, the bottle of milk and being 'hot' in bed.

I didn't tell my mother and father of the sleepover parties. I am only 5 but somehow I am aware that I don't feel comfortable talking about it. I don't know why, but Charlie says I can talk to him about it.

By this time, I had already missed a lot of school. I was always sick, being sent to stay with Doris during the school day when no one else was around. I enjoyed this special time. I was given lots of ice cream for my sore throats and taken to the local shop after lunch to buy a comic to read. I would snuggle up on the sofa with a blanket and bottle of warm milk and Doris would read stories to me and tell me how pretty I was. She would tell me how much she loved me and how much she wanted me to become part of her family. She said everything we did together was because of love, a special love that God wants us to feel. Little did I know that this was a dangerous love, a love that the Children of God cult preached about to millions worldwide.

I was too young to understand and knew that my mummy and daddy loved me so it must be ok for Doris to love me the way she did and to do those things to me and her children. After all, I was only a small child and wanted to please any adult that would show me kindness and affection. Doris said I could be her little princess in her family of love and that there were lots of other children that God had chosen to be part of this loving family.

It was after my fifth birthday that my sore throats and earaches got worse and I was told by my mother that I had to go into hospital for a little while to have my tonsils taken out.
I remember the white magic cream that the nurse put on my hands under a clear plaster. She said this was so the injections wouldn't hurt. Charlie sat on the bed with me whilst the doctor put the needle in my hand. The nurse was talking quietly to me as I drifted off into a deep sleep. This is how Lily an alter that came about because of the operation relates what happened:

'The sound in the room echoes as the machines tick on and off and doctors and nurses are scrubbing up. Nataley is asleep. She can't hear the noises in the room, or smell the disinfectant or feel the touch of their hands on her tiny body. I lay awake, listening and watching as the doctors put on their face masks and gloves and lift up my night shirt.

It hurts as they push the long shiny stick into me and move it around, faster and faster. They are smiling. One man is standing in the corner, watching. He breathes heavy as the bright light flashes on his camera. He moves to a different position, a better angle for his pictures. They are putting their fingers in now and twisting them round. My tummy feels like its on fire and I want to shout out. Please let them stop, I beg myself, please let them stop.

He climbs on to the bed, crushing my body whilst the nurse holds my head. His face is close to my closed eyes and his knees dig into my legs. The pain gets worse and the people are making animal noises as the man moves up and down my body. I can feel the blood running down my legs but I can't wipe it away. I'm frozen. I cry for Nataley.

She has escaped this for now, but one day I will have to tell her the secret, but for now she is safe.'

I can hear my mother talking gently to me, holding my hand and my father is sitting on the other side, with Susan on his knee.
'It's all over now. You did really well.'
'My throat hurts mummy' I say with a croak.
'Its ok, the nice lady said you can have some ice cream when you are a bit more awake. Then we can go home.'
On the way home from the hospital, my father stopped off at our local Woolworths store and bought Susan and I a bubble bear as a treat. I love my bear and hug him tight as we drive the short distance to our house.

I didn't have to go to school for a week following my small operation. This was great fun as my mother took the week off work to look after me and we spent every day the same. We would go out to the park in the morning, come home for lunch after feeding the ducks, then cuddle up under a duvet on the sofa whilst watching cartoon films. Charlie named my bubble bear fudge and from then on, he went everywhere with me and shared everything until I was about 12yrs old. Charlie made fudge talk and Susan and I played games with our bears, pretending they were real. It seems silly now, but at the time it gave us great comfort during the hard times of the abuse, that was still ongoing.

I was eager to get back to school after my week away and enjoyed the attention I got from my friends and teachers. They wanted to know all about my trip to hospital, so I told them in great detail, adding in a few extremes for effect. This wasn't the only operation I was to have. Over the next few years I had grommets put in my ears and taken out again, and when I was 9yrs old I had my appendix removed. This left my school friends totally jealous of the scar that appeared on my tummy. I even got two weeks off school for this operation and I didn't have to do any sport for six weeks!

Some of the earliest memories I have of school is playing with my friends. I had a lot of friends in my class and we would all sit together and play in the playground at lunch time.
I remember once, playing on the climbing frame and there was a boy who was about eleven years old that was picking on his little sister. He was being really nasty to her and I remember thinking to myself, 'I don't want him to hurt me.' So I laughed at the nasty things he was doing and started to join in with him. It felt really good not to be on the receiving end of the abuse and so I teamed up with him and became a bit of a bully myself. I would steal toys from children and call them horrible names. I would laugh at them when they got hurt by this older boy and I would encourage him to upset them more. This kept me away from the cruel things he would probably have done to me had I not taken his side.

One lunch time, I sneaked into the cloakroom and searched through the children's coat pockets. I found a toy plastic tiger and a medal of some sort. I quickly hid them in my coat and ran back to the playground where I put the medal round my neck. The next day, a dinner lady came up to me and asked me to unzip my jacket. In doing so, I revealed the beautiful shiny medal that I had stolen only the day before. I was marched off to the school headmasters office where my mother was called and I had to explain what I had done and I was sent home for the rest of the day, in shame. My mother was furious that I had done such a thing and sent me straight to bed without any tea. I felt awful. I was only six years old, however I knew right from wrong and could feel my face burn with embarrassment as she told my father when he got home from work.

Over the next few weeks, I continued to steal and to tease other children. I just couldn't help myself, it felt so good to do bad things to other people and not have them done to me. It became an obsession until one day I had a shock.

On this occasion, I had been doing naughty things all day. I had been in trouble for stealing some chalk from my teachers desk and writing bad words all over the walls. I had taken a smaller child's homework and ripped it up in front of him, making him burst into tears. Little did I know that this child's mother worked in the school and came and gave me a good talking to. However, I still didn't seem to care what I was doing and how hurtful I was being, until I got a taste of my own medicine so to speak.

I was in the playground with a group of friends when they all started laughing at me and pointing to my head. I became very cross when they wouldn't tell me what was so funny and I started to get upset that everyone in the group was looking and laughing at me. As I put my hand on my head to feel for whatever was so funny, a sharp pain went through my finger like burning fire. I screamed and looked at my hand to see the sting of a wasp sticking out of my finger! In panic, I wet myself right there in front of everyone, and yet again was subject to more laughing and teasing. I was in pain and felt so embarrassed to have wet myself. This truly was payback for all the nasty things and teasing I had done to everyone else. From that day, I didn't tease, steal or say nasty things to any of my friends again.

Another memory I have of school is of two boys that I became involved with. I was six years old and Lee and Darren were in my class.

It started one day when I was walking along the corridor on my way to lunch when Lee pulled up his tee-shirt to reveal his penis sticking out over his trousers. I didn't know what to do so ran away and hid in the cloakroom until he had gone. I was in shock. I had never seen boys bits before, even my dad covered up after a shower. I knew I shouldn't have seen it and decided it must have been an accident.

The next time I saw Lee, he did the same thing again, revealing himself to me and laughing. I ran and hid in the girls bathroom, thinking I was safe from yet another form of abuse. However, Lee had different ideas and came to the bathroom to find me. He pushed me into a cubicle and got his penis out again, rubbing it up and down my school dress. I started to cry and he put it away and quickly left the bathroom. This must be all my fault, I thought.

Once a week, we had video time in the afternoon for half an hour. I loved this time as we could mess around in the dark without our teachers knowing who was making the noise. I would sit next to my best friend Sarah and play around instead of watching the magic number episodes.

One day a boy called Darren came and sat next to me. No one really liked Darren. He smelled a bit and always had a runny nose that he would smear across his face. His hair was scruffy and his clothes always looked and smelled dirty. I felt a bit sorry for him as he didn't have many friends and used to live with his nana as he was taken away from his parents. I found out later, when I was much older that this was due to physical and sexual abuse from his father.

Anyway, during the film, Darren started to tickle me on my ankle, just above my sock. It felt really nice so I let him carry on. He didn't say anything, just kept stroking my ankle, then the bottom of my thigh. From then on, every video time, as soon as the lights went out, Darren would tickle and stroke my legs, until one day he got braver. I was sitting crossed legged so my dress was just hanging in my lap. He started to stroke my leg and gradually moved his hand up to the top of my thigh, right by my knickers. He then stroked me, over my knickers between my legs. I froze. What was he doing? Doris had done this to me countless times and I knew I didn't feel comfortable with it. Should I shout or stay still? Terrified, I stayed totally still and allowed him to slip his hands into my knickers and stroke me between the legs. He started to hurt me as he put his finger inside and moved it really fast. I could feel his sharp fingernail scratching my insides. I started to cry and Darren pulled his hand away. My teacher asked me what was going on and I told her I didn't feel very well.

My mother came to collect me from school that day and I was obviously very upset at what had just happened to me. She asked me what was wrong. I couldn't tell on an adult like Doris could I? But I certainly could tell on a child. It didn't seem so threatening to tell what a child had done to me. So I told her how it had started with just a tickle, then a stroke and then how he had put his hands in my knickers. My mother was furious and went straight over to Darren and his nana and a lot of shouting took place. My class teacher was bought in on the conversation and after that day, I didn't see Darren anymore. He must have moved schools I thought.

'I am lying in my bed drifting off to sleep. Nataley is already asleep, snoring heavily. We have been off school today because she isn't well again. I wriggle around, trying to get comfortable. Something doesn't feel right, I can sense the monsters coming.

I hear a noise at the window and shut my eyes tight. Nataley doesn't know about the monsters that visit her regularly. They are big and mean and like to upset us little ones.
They open the bedroom window and I hear them growling and breathing heavy all over me. They are standing over our bed. A giant claw reaches down and hurls us into a cage. Then, out of the window we go, through the sky and into some sort of room. There are lots of

monsters here. I'm very scared. Please don't wake up Nataley, I don't want you to see this. I have to be brave for her.

The monster with the claw hangs the giant bird like cage from the ceiling of the dark room and scurries off into the corner. I cover my eyes with my hands and my blanket and listen to the grunts and growls from these beasts.

The door to the cage opens and I feel an icy cold presence enter. It is inserted trough my mouth and travels into my left arm. I can feel its heavy, dark, evil presence in me. The tracking device is inserted, along with a monster to keep it safe.

I open one eye and see the tall bony lady standing there, watching. Her eyes are red like fire, piercing the darkness. They burn into me as the cage is closed again and I fly high up into the sky once more.

Back in our room, it is cold and damp and the air smells musty. I can hear the sound of Nataley, still snoring. My arm hurts. It feels like it has been frozen. I look at it. There is no mark, just the memory of my alien encounter.'

I was seven years old when this happened to me. I believe what Kai (an alter) has told me. He came along and saved me from this awful haunting. Some people will not believe that aliens or monsters exist in our world, but they do. I should know, I have seen them, felt them and had them touch me. That afternoon whilst I was sleeping, they grabbed me from my bed, under the orders of Doris and inserted a detection device so she could keep tabs on me. I'm sure the cult she was involved with have done this to many young innocent children over the years. Perhaps she is still doing it. The device is used to control the monsters within the child and to allow others to enter.

.Like Charlie and lily, their stories are true as they can't lie. They are here to protect me and allow me to carry on with life, away from the horrible memories of abuse.

Kai's story shows the extreme evil that we are living with every day. There is no limit to the amount of evil that can be done to an unprotected child by an adult who is under demonic influence. This true story proves that nothing should be overlooked when dealing with such evil.

By the time I had just turned nine years old, my father was made redundant and so was looking for work. My parents decided to relocate to Margate in Kent where my grandparents were living. For months we travelled back and forth from London to Margate looking for a place to live, whilst my dad was having interviews for new jobs. Eventually, we found a lovely three bedroom house by the seafront. The plan was to move into the new home in September.

I remember the move as though it were yesterday. Susan and I attended the local Salvation Army youth club on the Friday night after our last day at school. Our parents picked us up in the car and we drove the two hour journey to Margate. We drove almost all the way, totally silent and I cried silent tears for my friends and my home back in London. I didn't want to move house. I was leaving behind lots of friends and in a strange way, I found it hard to leave Doris and the abuse. It was like I was conditioned into being abused and was frightened at the prospect of having a normal life away from it all. After all, Doris had said that she was showing me a special love from god and that I was one of the lucky children to be receiving such love.

When we arrived in Margate, we stayed with my grandparents for the night and in the morning Susan and I were told that my mother and father had to go back to London to pack up the house and move our belongings into the new one. Once again I cried as I didn't want to be left with my grandparents even if it was only for the week.

That week is a blur of sleepless nights and boring days. We didn't really get on with our grandparents. My grandfather was quite funny and made us laugh with his silly jokes but my grandmother was a very stern and frightening lady to a small child. She didn't make us feel very welcome and didn't do anything to occupy our time. She was more interested in sitting in her armchair listening to the radio that my granddad would only allow on at certain times. We weren't allowed to watch the television and we didn't have many of our toys to play with either. As you can imagine, we were very bored and depressed the whole time we were there and so we got very excited the next weekend when our mother came to collect us.

Our new house was just in the next town to where my grandparents were living. As we drove there, I could see and smell the sea that was just around the corner from our new house. I began to get very excited and thought that maybe this wasn't so bad after all.

Susan and I raced up the garden drive and into the house. We ran upstairs to find our new bedrooms. Disappointment overcame me as I sat on my bed looking at my room. This wasn't my room. I couldn't imagine how it could ever be my room. The carpet was dirty and smelly and the wallpaper was old fashioned with large flowers all over it. However, I had my own sink and my window looked out onto the beautiful large garden with a massive pond. The pond had a water fountain that was running clear sparkly water and I could just about see a few tiny gold fish swimming around. This I thought, was o.k.

My parents examined the house from top to bottom and by the time dark fell, they decided it was not going to be suitable to live in straight away. My father was extremely sad at what he found. We had left behind a beautiful four bedroom house in London for this. There was grease all over the kitchen, flies hovering around in every room, dirt up the walls, the floors were sticky, all the cables and phone lines had been cut, there were cigarette burn marks in the carpets and the worst of all was to be found. My dad checked out the small downstairs toilet, only to find it was totally full of dog poo! The smell was awful and there were flies everywhere. I think that night was the first time I had ever seen my father cry. What had we done?

So for two weeks whilst my father cleaned and sorted the house out so we could at least live in it whist it was being redecorated, we lived in our caravan that was in a park close by. This was quite fun as I had always enjoyed our holidays in this static home. Eventually though, it came to an end and we moved into the new house that was much cleaner and looked slightly more homely.

Over the next few weeks, we unpacked our belongings and made our house into our home. My father decorated our bedrooms and worked really hard on the kitchen and bathroom to make them more usable. Susan and I explored our surroundings and played hide and seek in the front and back gardens every day. However, we were getting bored and it was time to start our new schools.

When we first arrived in Margate, my dad still hadn't found a job and we didn't have a school to go to. The school that my parents wanted us to attend could only offer us one space and so it was decided that my parents would home tutor us until places became available in the local primary school.

My parents tried really hard to amuse and entertain us during planned lessons by my father but it was no use. We were both bored and needed to be with other children. So we started the following week at our local Junior and infant school. I didn't like this school at all and was glad when my parents got a phone call to say we could both start on Monday morning at the local church school. This was the school that we all liked and my parents were overjoyed that they had managed to find us a place.

We had been living in Margate now for about a month when my mother got a phone call one Saturday morning to say that my granddad had been taken to hospital with a suspected heart attack. So that morning, she went to be with him in the hospital and my father, Susan and I went to the local shops. When we arrived home, we noticed that our back door was open and we had been burgled. All of our cupboards and draws were open and my mothers jewellery box was left on the floor, completely empty. My father phoned my mother who rushed home from the hospital and arrived at the same time as the local police.

That night my little sister and I slept in the same bed together as we were so frightened that the burglar would come back and hurt us. We stayed awake most of the night, listening to the noises outside on the main road. Every sound made us jump and cuddle each other. We held each other close like we used to do during our visits to Doris's house. I remember her showing us the proper way to kiss each other. We would be told to open our mouths and touch tongues and Doris would show us how to do it and then once we had got it right she would smile and tell us to hold still whilst she took a photo of us intimately kissing.

We hadn't done anything like that since moving away, until the night we shared a bed. Susan kissed me and rubbed her body up and down mine. I remember a warm feeling down below as she did this and I started to tingle all over. This was the feeling I got when Doris would touch me down below. I would get hot and my body would tingle. This feeling became normal to the both of us and so Susan and

I carried this behaviour on as though it were a normal thing to do between two sisters. We had never heard of the word incest before.

A couple of months after the burglary, we were invited to a big family party back up in London. There was loads of friends and family there that I had never even met before and it was good fun catching up with old relatives.

I enjoyed the disco that was there and went off on my own to dance. When I turned round to find my parents and brother and sisters, they were gone. I couldn't see them anywhere and began to panic, thinking they had gone home without me!

Eventually, I spotted my brother who was across the dark room. He took me to my mother who was crying in the corridor outside. I didn't know what had happened but she told me we were going home. I said goodbye to my older brother and sister and got in the car, feeling very frightened. Nobody said a word for at least a few miles into our journey back to Margate.
'What's wrong mum?' I asked. She didn't answer.
It was Susan that filled me in on the details on the way home.

My dad had gone to the toilet and whilst he was washing his hands, my uncle, who was a complete psycho, jumped on him and beat him up. He told my dad that he knew where we lived and that he had burgled our house and taken all my mothers jewellery. As he bashed my dad's head against the toilet sink, he said if we told anyone he would kill us all. Obviously, my father was frightened by this attack and so, telling my grandmother what a dangerously disturbed man she was allowing into the family, we left the party. I was in shock. I think I cried all the way home and when I saw my dad's bruises on his body I cried even more for I was scared for us all. I realised that night, that nothing in my family was ever normal, and this was just the beginning of it all.

After the attack on my father, Susan and I started to relive some of the horrors that went on in Doris's care. We thought it was normal to touch and play with each other and eventually we were doing this on a regular basis. One of us would lay on the bed and the other would pretend to be a doctor and touch the others body. Then we would kiss and cuddle for ages. Doris had taught us that this was right and that we should show each other love like this all the time. We were just carrying on with what had been drummed into us the first part of our young lives.

It wasn't long before the sexual abuse came out in our everyday play. My bubble bear fudge would be used as a prop in a role play of the things that had happened to us. We would pretend that we were the abusers and that we were doing all those horrible things to him. I think by playing these games, it allowed us to come to terms with what had been done to us. This was when Maisy arrived. Susan and I developed a special bond between us that we called Maisy. She was our saviour, a friend to hide behind when things got too much to handle in our own minds. I was 10 years old when she arrived and every day she would take over at some point and play with Susan like best friends. They would try make up on, play with our toys and laugh and fool around all the time. Sometimes, Susan would be Maisy and play games with me and be my best friend. She helped us block out all those bad memories of what we had done together, to each other and she allowed us to be children for a short time again.

During this time of my life, I made a very special and close friend also by the name of Jane. Unfortunately we are no longer in contact. Jane was the sister of Susans best friend Mary. We all played together in and out of primary school and used to sleep round each others houses at the weekend. We also joined the same karate club and so spent almost all of our time together. Their parents were very relaxed when it came to what we were allowed to do when we slept at their house and this is when I had my first taste of alcohol, which I hated!

Between the four of us, we formed a special group and called it the 'boogley gang.' We were all given a special name and mine was 'Jeeckey', Susans was 'Goldfish', Jane was 'Boogley' and Mary was 'Boogley eye'. We had so much fun, playing tricks on each other and getting into trouble for the silly things we used to do. As we all lived on the sea front, we spent the whole school holidays down on the beach and climbing on top of the beach huts, just messing around. Susan and I lived near to a small green area and we used to hang out down there too, climbing trees and hiding in the bushes, pretending to find things that belonged to the local tramps. It was great fun.

However, we did do bad things aswell. I can remember staying over at their house for the weekend. We watched a horror movie called "*The Shining*" and then spent the rest of the night petrified! One night, Jane had the great idea to try levitation. We took it in turns to lay on the bedroom floor whilst the other three of us would touch the person laying on the floor with only one finger. Then we would chant something along the lines of 'make this person fly' and we would wait to see if they moved off the ground. We never imagined it would actually work! But one day it did. Susan rose off the floor for a few seconds and we all freaked out. As we screamed she slammed back down onto the ground, we were all totally shaken up. Never again did we try this.

We did perform other types of black magic though. I don't know who came up with these ideas but it always ended in tears so to speak. Another game we would play was called black widow. We would stand in front of a mirror and on the stroke of midnight we would say black widow seven times. On one particular night we were in my bedroom and we were playing these games. I looked into the mirror and said very quietly black widow seven times. On the seventh time I laughed as nothing happened. The game says a black witch is supposed to stare back at you and jump out of the mirror. Nothing happened. Or so I thought. When we eventually decided to go to sleep, I couldn't sleep. I kept feeling as though I was being watched. I got up out of bed and went over to the mirror and there staring back at me was a black creepy shadow of what looked like an old lady! I screamed so loudly that I woke my parents up and got into lots of trouble for playing such dangerous games. I don't however, think that my parents or Jane, Mary and Susan believed me.

After this event, we became more and more interested in the occult. Jane came up with the idea of doing the Ouija board. She wanted to contact her nana that had recently died and so we decided to give it a go.

Jane and Mary came over to our house and we sat in my bedroom and made the board. We cut out all the letters and stuck them on to a piece of card board. Then, when my parents went out we found a glass and sat round the kitchen table.

We all put our hands on the glass and said very clearly, 'is anybody there?' Nothing happened. We tried again, 'is anybody there?' Again nothing happened until the third time. We asked again and this time the glass slowly moved. We all pulled our hands away and gave a frightened laugh. Once getting over the shock and excitement, we tried again. This time we asked for Jane and Mary's nana to come forward. Silence. Then BANG! The kitchen door slammed and the glass flew off the table and smashed on the floor! We all shot up the stairs as a man appeared at the window. This would be the man that would haunt me for many years after.

After the incident with the Ouija board, I became almost obsessed with the occult and Satanism. I looked it up on the internet and bought my own Ouija board and satanic bible. I would carry this bible everywhere with me, frightened that my parents would find it. I even became friends with two boys at school that were known Satanists. I was totally hooked.

Even though I was interested in the Occult, I was also very frightened. The man who appeared when we did the Ouija board stayed with me. He would follow me everywhere. He was at my house, in my garden and he even went to school with me. I didn't have a clue who this person was but I did know that he was very scary and when he started to talk to me, I had to listen.

One day when I was 14 years old, he appeared walking up the road past my school. I saw him coming and tried to run away and hide. I even told one of my friends what was happening and she told me to go to the school counsellor.

He followed me into the play ground and told me to find a group of children that were older than me. When I had found them I was to ask for a special package. This package contained the drug amphetamine. So, I did as I was told. I went over to this group who were sitting on the grass and spoke to the leader. He gave me a handful of pills and I put them in my pocket. Racing to the toilets, I took all of them on the mans commands and immediately I felt sick. What had I done? I knew it was wrong to take drugs but how could I go against this man? Everything started spinning and I couldn't walk in a straight line. I had to miss all my afternoon lessons and sit in the toilets until I got the bus home at the end of the day. Once home I went straight to bed and slept it off.

It was that night that I told my boyfriend what was going on. His name was Chris and to this day we are still together, married with two beautiful children.

I told him how we had played with a Ouija board a few months before and how the man had appeared but no one else could see him and how he follows me every where and makes me do things. If I don't do what he says, I will burn in hell and Satan will punish me for eternity!

Chris listened as I cried over the phone and told me that he knew who the man was and what I needed to do to get rid of him. He told me that the man was an evil spirit that had come through the Ouija board and that I had to get rid of him. The only way to do this was to talk to Jesus about it and ask for forgiveness for all the bad things I have done. Jesus? I thought. What on earth has he got to do with it? Why should I say sorry to him for having fun? Its none of his business what I get up to.

Although I went to church and called myself a Christian, I wasn't. I didn't pray or read the bible and I certainly didn't live like a Christian. I was doing drugs, stealing, getting drunk on a regular basis and practicing the occult. That certainly wasn't a Christian life. Any way, things got so bad that I decided to try Jesus. I even told my mother what was happening and she said that I had to pray hard for forgiveness. So, I tried to pray and read my Bible. Every time I tried to pray, bad thoughts came into my head and it was impossible to think. Every time I tried to read the Bible, the words kept getting mixed up and I couldn't see to read it! It was no use, I just couldn't do it. Chris tried to help me over the phone by telling me what to say in the prayers but I found an excuse every time not to say them and I had a problem with saying the word 'Jesus'. I just physically could not say it! After weeks of trying, nothing had changed and so Chris decided that I needed extra help from the church. He went to speak to the minister of the church, Arthur.

That evening, I was down at the church after singing practice with the choir. I went into the kitchen to get a drink of water and a man that I knew had died a few months ago, appeared, surrounded by flames. His face was grey and you could see his cheek bones through his skin. I was so frightened and to this day I have never forgotten that awful sight. I ran upstairs in floods of tears and told Chris what I had just seen. He went straight to Arthur. Unfortunately, Arthur was the wrong person to tell. He called me in to his office and asked me what I was seeing and asked me about the man that follows me around and about playing the Ouija board. I told him everything. I thought I could trust him and that being the minister of the church, he would help me. I was wrong. He told me I was sick and needed to see a doctor. He said I was experiencing psychotic episodes and that these things weren't real! With that, he dismissed me from his office. So that was it, I was going mad! Chris didn't think he was right and still told me that I needed proper help from a deliverance minister, to get rid of the man. He was going to go against Arthur and get me the help I so desperately needed. It would be hard though as no-one believed me. I later found out that Arthur had called a meeting and told every one in the church that I was mad and to keep away from me and to not listen to me. I believe now that he was frightened of the unknown.

It was around this time that I had some very bad news. My mother had been diagnosed with breast cancer, a very rare form of it and she was to have lots of treatment in hospital. The whole family was devastated but I remember my mother saying to Susan and I, *'this doesn't mean I'm going to die.'* When you hear the word cancer, people just assume that that is the end, the person will die. But my parents ensured me that she was going to receive treatment and in a few months everything will be back to normal.

That night, I lay in my bed crying and crying. I was very frightened of all the things that were happening in my life. I was on drugs, into the occult, had the man following and tormenting me all the time, I had the awful memories of the sexual abuse I had suffered and now my mother was terminally ill. How did things get so bad? Why are they happening to me?

I was convinced that I was being punished by God for all the bad things I had done. That must be the reason he was taking the one thing I loved so much away from me. She had cancer, so she was going to die, I was convinced.

So, with nowhere to turn to, I began to pray to Satan. Surely he would help me and give me some answers? No, he just abused me even more. Under his instructions, I took a penknife to my arm and began to cut the flesh. The skin broke and the blood began to flow. The pain was great! It felt as though I was in control and everything that was going wrong in my life was just washed away with my blood. It felt good and I liked it.

After I had cut myself a few times I felt ashamed at the way it looked and began to cry again. Charlie comforted me and told me it would all be ok. He helped me clean my arm up and talked to me all night until I eventually fell into a troublesome sleep.

In the morning my arm looked a mess, but I was pleased with the feeling I got and that I had taken control of something in my life.

Chris was very upset with what I had done. He said it was a very bad thing to do and that I was opening doors to let more evil spirits into my life. I thought ' what on earth is he on about?'

Anyway, he was determined to help me and decided to talk to a lady at our church who he knew was into deliverance and would listen to me.

Sandra, a very quiet but friendly lady, picked me and my mother up in her car and drove us to a church in the next town. There, after the meeting, I was going to meet with some other people for prayer. My mother was also going to receive prayer from the pastor to help her get better.

Sitting in the meeting, I was so nervous. I didn't have a clue what these people were going to do. Would they say I had the devil in me and there was no hope? Would they believe the story I had to tell or would they just laugh and say I was making it all up? I was terrified.

After the service, Sandra introduced me to an older couple called Doug and Berol who were going to talk to me and pray for me. We went into a back room in the church and sat down. They introduced themselves and asked me lots of questions about myself. I began to tell them the story of my life. Looking at me in horror, they sat there, totally silent. When I had finished talking they asked if they could pray for me. I agreed and Doug put some sort of oil on my head in the form of a cross. Then he began to pray. I felt sick. The room began to spin and I wanted to shout something but my vocal chords wouldn't work. I could hear screaming in my head and voices around the room that didn't belong to Doug or Berol, talking to me. My whole body began to shiver and I felt cold deep inside me. The next thing I remember is Doug smiling at me and reassuring me that I didn't have any evil spirits in me and that I was quite normal. Feeling very odd I quickly left the room to go and find my mum. She was sitting in the pews with a lady, chatting. Berol came up to my mother and put her arm round her and said a quick prayer. We then left and Berol gave me a bible to keep with her mobile number inside, to contact her or Doug if I needed to talk about anything.

I couldn't get out of that church quick enough. All the way home I sat silently, thinking about what had happened, about the oil on my head, the screaming and the voices and what Doug had said about me not having evil spirits in me. Nothing made sense, and when I told Chris, he thought their opinion was wrong. What's wrong with me then? What does all this mean?

Feeling hopeless, I began to cut myself again. The pain made the whole evening disappear and for a while I could forget what had happened that night at the church.

After the meeting with Doug and Berol, things began to get a lot worse. The man was tormenting me day and night and I found that I was unable to function normally. I couldn't sleep, I didn't eat much and I was finding school work hard to keep up with. My mind was constantly on the occult and the man and I didn't think about anything else. Even when I did sleep, I had terrible nightmares.

My dad decided to take me to see our local doctor as I couldn't sleep. The doctor asked me lots of questions and I didn't really say much to him. He sent me for an appointment with a child play therapist to see if they could help me.

During my visits to the play therapist we would talk about family life and my mother being diagnosed with cancer. She decided that I was suffering from depression due to the stress of my mother being sick, so referred me to a psychiatrist. He put me on anti depressants and I had to go and see him every week after school. My father became very worried as I wouldn't tell him what was wrong. I just kept saying that I was having nightmares about mum. This was true to a point, however I couldn't tell him about the abuse and about the things I was getting involved in. I don't know why, but I think I was just too embarrassed and wasn't sure if he would believe all the stuff about the occult. My dad wasn't religious at all and talking to him about religion and Jesus and Satan would just make my life worse. So I continued to take my medication and get on with my life the way it was. But things were about to change. I was about to find the one person who could help me.

My mother became increasingly unwell over the next few months and subsequently my behaviour got worse. I was cutting myself on a regular basis now, even sneaking off to the school toilets during lessons to do it! I became totally obsessed with cutting and learning about the occult. However, I didn't want to be like this. I wanted to be normal again, I wanted all the pain to go away. Chris kept on about deliverance and so I checked it out on the internet. Lots of websites came up but one stood out in particular. This website was about a man named Jay, who was an exorcist and healer. His website stated that *'Exorcism is a labour of love to free someone from an evil spirit.'* I decided to contact him. Even though he lived in America, he could perhaps email me and give me some answers as to how to get rid of the man. It was worth a try. So I emailed him asking him for help.

'Hi, my name is Nataley and I live in England. I need some help. I did the Ouija board and now a man keeps following me and won't leave me alone. Is this an evil spirit?'

I waited and waited for a response but none came. So I forgot about Jay and exorcisms. I thought it was a bit silly anyway, contacting someone for help that lived that far away! I didn't believe anyone could help me now.

I was in bed one night when I heard my mother and father coming up the stairs. My mother was very ill at this point and found it very hard to walk. My father was helping her up the stairs. I could hear her puffing and panting as she tried to climb the stairs to bed. The sound of this made me cry as I knew it wouldn't be long before she was to die.

Two personalities by the names of Natty and Rosie arrived that night. They were very upset and angry that my mother was dying and took on all the pain that I was suffering. Every time I heard my mother cry or be sick, Natty and Rosie came up to protect me from the awful feelings I was experiencing. Just like Charlie, Maisy, Lily, Kai and Darren, they were there to help me through this part of my life that I was finding so hard to deal with.

May 2003, my mother took a turn for the worst and ended up in a hospice. Once in there I knew she would never come out. The cancer had spread to her lungs and her blood and so there was no more treatment she could have. It was just a waiting game now, waiting for her to finally give up the fight and die.

Chris and I had booked to go to a Christian conference for the bank holiday weekend, which was also my sixteenth birthday. I knew how sick my mother was but still wanted to go. I don't think I realised just how imminent her death was. I went to visit her the night before I went away. She didn't even recognise me! The nurses said it was because of all the pain killers she was taking. I just remember her looking at me blankly, and asking my dad to help her out of bed to use the toilet.

At the end of the visit, mum remembered who I was and gave me a kiss on the cheek and told me to have a good time at the conference. As I walked away, I could see a tear roll down her cheek. She must have known that was the last time we would see each other. They say that people know when they are going to die, and I think she did.

On the first night I was at the conference, my younger sister phoned me. She had been to see my mother and told me that she was very ill and that the doctors said she didn't have long left to live. I was hundreds of miles away and couldn't make it home in time to see her. I felt awful. What if she died before I was due to return home? I didn't get a chance to say I loved her or goodbye!

That night I lay in my tent, unable to sleep. When I finally did fall asleep, the monsters visited me. They showed me pictures of my mother lying in a bed with her skin on her face peeling off and crows pecking at her eyes. They told me she was dying and I couldn't get to her.

I had only been awake from my nightmare an hour or two when my father called to give me the bad news that she had passed away early that morning. I took the call very calmly and told Chris what had happened. He didn't know what to say. I think he expected me to break down in tears, but I had no emotional reaction at all.

I carried on for the rest of the weekend as though nothing had happened until the last night when I finally broke down. I cried in my tent for what seemed like hours. I didn't get to say goodbye, I kept saying over and over in my head. How could I be so selfish and go away to a Christian conference knowing that my mother was terminally ill and needed me? I had the horrible image of her in my head that the demons put there the night before. They made me watch her die.

The next morning I packed up my things and we travelled back to Kent. When I arrived home, the place looked and felt empty, even though there were lots of people there. My older brother and sister had come to stay until the funeral and my dad and younger sister were there too, waiting for me. Standing round the kitchen table, I opened my birthday presents and cards in silence. Then I went to bed. In the morning I went to school as normal and my dad went to work. Nothing about my mum was mentioned.

The funeral was two weeks later and there were lots and lots of people there. I was furious that Arthur was to conduct the funeral after the way he had treated me. But my dad said that was what she had wanted.

After the funeral, I decided to sort myself out. I couldn't continue the way I was and my mum would have been upset to know how frightened and alone I felt. I didn't want to be like this anymore and so I agreed to meet with a guy called Jeremy, who was one of Chris' friends.

Chris and I travelled up to Yorkshire on the Friday night and stayed in a friends house. In the morning we were to meet with Jeremy and Alan at Jeremy's house.

On the way to his house I was again, really nervous. Would he believe me? And more importantly, would he be able to help me? These were questions that I kept asking myself on the short journey to his house. When we arrived, I couldn't even look at him. I kept hiding behind Chris. I didn't know why I was hiding but now I believe it was the demons that were hiding from him, they couldn't look a man of God in the face.

Jeremy told Chris and his friend Kurt to go upstairs and pray whilst him and Alan were to do the deliverance with me. We were going to go through a book called *"10 steps to freedom"* by Neil Anderson.

Jeremy got me to tick off all the things I had been involved in, even the things my parents were involved in, including the Freemasons, which my dad was part of. Then we had to pray and ask for forgiveness for each occult practice I had been involved in and renounce it.

Here came the problem. I was unable to say the word 'Jesus'. Every time I tried to say it, nothing came out of my mouth. I almost felt very frightened to say it! Jeremy and Alan stared at me. I began to get nervous and started to self harm. I bit my hand so hard that I could taste the blood in my mouth. This is when Jeremy turned nasty. He shouted at me and told me that I didn't want his help and that it was a waste of time helping me. This wasn't true! I did want his help, but I couldn't say that word. He told me that he was going upstairs and until I decided to say Jesus, he was going to lock me in the room on my own. I was petrified! Him and Alan left the room, and the voices started talking to me. I could hear the screaming in my head again and I was shaking all over. Don't leave me on my own! Please somebody stay with me! The demons arrived and tormented me for hours.

The meeting with Jeremy and Alan didn't work. I wasn't able to say the name Jesus and I didn't get the help I so desperately needed. Jeremy turned out to be a bad idea and I believe he made things worse. I lost trust in people who said they believed me and wanted to help. I even lost trust in Chris.

Once I was back home, I decided to give Jay another try. I emailed him again asking for help and telling him what Jeremy and Alan had done to me. He emailed me straight back! I was excited as I hadn't expected to hear from him at all. He said that what they had done was wrong and that I did need help to get rid of the evil spirits. He also said that he would ring me and talk to me about everything! I just couldn't believe it. Someone, thousands of miles away believed me and wanted to help me!

A few weeks later, I was at Chris' house and Jay phoned me. We spoke for over an hour about my life and the things that were happening to me. At the end of the conversation, Jay said a prayer and told me Jesus was going to set me free. He also took my address and said he was going to send me a DVD of an exorcism he had performed whilst visiting Germany.

When I received the DVD, I couldn't believe what I was watching. Jay was giving a talk to a group of young people on Jesus, demons and deliverance. He spoke about all the experiences he had had and then invited the group to pray out loud for salvation and deliverance. A few minutes into prayer and a young boy started to make animal noises and roll around the floor! Jay immediately went over to him and the demons inside him became angry and violent as Jay read the bible and asked them who they were and what right they had to the young boy.

After a long fight, the young boy was healed and the demons were gone. He looked so happy and testified of what Jesus had done for him. I was totally amazed and also a bit frightened. What I had just seen looked a bit scary but I was also interested in how Jay worked and what Jesus had done for this boy. I decided then and there that I wanted to meet with Jay to find liberation from the things that were tormenting me.

It was a very cold night at the beginning of March 2004. The snow had blocked all the roads off and everything was covered in ice. We were due to meet with Jay and his wife in their hotel room in London. They had flown all the way from Dallas for the weekend to meet with me for prayer. They really wanted to help me! I still couldn't quite believe what was happening.

Chris and I waited at the front of the hotel and Jay arrived to meet us. He came up to me and immediately I felt at ease as he had a big smile and was very friendly.

Up in the hotel room I met Jay's wife. She too was very friendly and welcoming and we talked for a while about their trip to London. Then Jay began to ask me questions about myself and the things that had been happening. I told him all the bad things I had done, about the drugs and Satanism and cutting myself. He listened and didn't judge me. He just kept saying that Jesus would forgive me and that he loved me. I couldn't quite believe this. How could I love someone and they love me when we hadn't even met? I told Jay what I was thinking and he asked me if I was a Christian. He then led me through a prayer and right there on that night, I became a Christian.

I remember Jay saying to me 'Nataley, just say Jesus.' But I couldn't! The more I tried the more I could hear voices screaming and shouting at me.

Jay placed a bible on my head and began to pray. The voices got louder and Jay's voice seemed to be in the distance. After that I went into a demon induced coma and don't remember anything that happened.

This is what Jay said about the deliverance :

A young woman, from London, England, by the name of Jenny reached out to us via our web ministry some years ago and inquired about receiving spiritual help from the evil spirits that had been tormenting her. Only 17 years old Jenny had already endured enough terror for a lifetime; years of satanic bondage, addiction to self mutilation, childhood sexual abuse, Dissociation, cultic brainwashing, and numerous emotional ills. Knowing she had not surrendered her life to Jesus, we began to pray for her salvation. Shortly thereafter, God answered our prayers and Jenny prayed to receive Christ into her life as Lord. She was now a child of God. Yet her torments were not over. The next step was to liberate her from tormenting spirits and to this end we began to pray. Jenny's problems were so intense it seemed necessary to work with her in person. Our prayers were soon answered when God graciously allowed my wife and me to travel to England to visit her.

The weeks leading up to the meeting were spiritually intense. Daily, we received death threats from the evil spirits that controlled this suffering woman. They arrived via e-mail, yet my wife and I continued to persevere, knowing that God would use us to cast out these very spirits.

When we arrived in the United Kingdom we set immediately to work. Over a course of three days we spent 20 hours battling demonic spirits. Soon into our work a powerful demon called "Death" came forward. When he manifested in Jenny her eyes rolled back in her head revealing only the whites of the eye; taking on a hideous look of death.

We confronted the demon in the power of the Holy Spirit; reading Sacred Scriptures and calling upon the angels of God to torment the demons by singing praises to God. This spiritual pressure drove the evil spirit to supernaturally raise Jenny from her chair and cause her to walk towards the bathroom in our hotel room. As she entered the bathroom the demon of death caused a paralysis to constrict her body. Completely unable to move the demon took control of her young body; she quickly lapsed into a demonized coma state.

In the power of God and through His holy angels we commanded the paralysis to cease. For an alarming period of time there was no response. She lay as one struck dead. The minimal rise and fall of her breathing were all that assured us she was alive. Undaunted, we continued to pray and storm heaven when suddenly she began to move ever so slightly. In Jesus name we commanded the paralysis to be lifted from her and God answered our prayer. Very slowly she began to walk; taking some thirty minutes to move just fifteen steps. But she walked. Jenny answered the call to walk just as Aeneas of old answered this same call from Peter:

Now it came to pass, as Peter went through all parts of the country, that he also came down to the saints who dwelt in Lydda. There he found a certain man named Aeneas, who had been bedridden eight years and was paralyzed. And Peter said to him, "Aeneas, Jesus the Christ heals you. Arise and make your bed." Then he arose immediately. (Acts 9:32-34)

After Jay and Elizabeth's visit, I immediately felt much better. I didn't get involved with drugs anymore and more importantly, the man that had been tormenting me had completely disappeared. However, there was still work to be done and Chris and I decided eventually we would go over to America to complete the deliverance.

Even though Jay had taken away a lot of demons from me, there were still some there which were tormenting me. I was still interested in the occult and would go on a website called occult forums every day. I became completely obsessed with the website and began to talk to Satanists in their online chat room. That is how I met Rob and Kyle.

Rob lived in Dallas and practiced witchcraft. He believed he was a shaman healer and said he could visit me supernaturally to heal me from the grief of my mother and the nightmares I was suffering from. Of course, I so desperately wanted to be healed that I took him up on this offer. Even though Jay had warned me about the occult, a demon convinced me that this was the only way to find relief from the pain and grief that I felt. So, I allowed Rob to astral project to my bedroom. It happened late one night when I was lying in my bed. Rob appeared at my bedside and put his hands on my head. We didn't talk but I could sense his presence and hear him mumbling some strange words in a language I couldn't understand. He said he was praying for me to be healed. After about 5mins, Rob disappeared into thin air and I was left alone again. I felt odd. What just happened was a bit scary and I didn't feel as though it had done me any good. I still felt devastated that my mother had passed away and my mind was filled with the horrible thoughts of her death.

Rob contacted me via email the next day and asked me how I felt. He said that it hadn't worked because he was getting bad vibes from me when he put his hands on my head. He said I would need a good few more visits from him to complete the healing.

So for the next few weeks, Rob came to my bedroom and layed his hands on me. Each time was the same and after a month or so, he didn't come anymore. I emailed him and asked him why he wasn't visiting me any more. He said his work with me was done. But I didn't feel any better, if anything I was feeling worse with every visit! That was the last I heard of him.

Kyle was a Satanist living in Liverpool, England. He was really friendly and sent me a picture of himself. He asked for a picture of me so I sent him one of me and Chris. A little while later I received an email from him saying he wanted another picture of me, but with no clothes on. I was totally shocked by this! After all the abuse I had gone through I was determined to never let anyone use me in that way again. I told him I wasn't going to send him a picture and that we should stop talking. However, demons were at work.

I was talking on the internet to Kyle one night when he mentioned the subject of sexual magic. Having never heard of this before, I was interested to hear what he had to say. He said that he practiced sexual magic and that's why he wanted a naked photo of me, to help him with his rituals. He told me that sexual magic gave you power and that demons helped you to fulfill all your dreams. I didn't quite understand what it all meant but I continued the conversation. He began to ask me intimate questions about myself. He asked if I masturbated and how often I did it. He asked how I pleased myself and if I was using this energy successfully. He said that by masturbating, you build up energy and you have to give it to your named demon in order to receive power. He showed me a picture of a sigil (a symbol created for the purpose of magic) and told me what to do with it. I won't go into details here, but reading between the lines, one can imagine what I had to do. Then I was to conjure a demon.

Kyle taught me how to conjure a demon and I read on the internet and in my satanic bible how to go about it. I was in a demonized trance. I wanted to meet my demon.

Slaanesh was a very powerful and determined demon. He was a demon of sexual pleasure and made me do things on a daily basis. He gave me the power to control people and to know things that others couldn't possibly know. He was a very high ranking demon, and you didn't want to get on the wrong side of him. I had to obey his every command and if I didn't, he said he would send a bigger, and more powerful demon to torment and destroy me. I was very frightened of him. Slanesh even carved his name into my arm one night, to prove to me that he was the owner of my soul and that I bowed down to him.

I couldn't take it any more and told Kyle I wanted out. I didn't want this demon anymore. He told me that you cant get rid of a demon once you have them as they own you.

Over the months, Slaanesh became even more demanding and powerful and he made me do really bad things. I was made to take and send naked and intimate pictures of myself to Kyle and other members of the forum. Kyle sent them to other Satanists and said that they would use them for their satanic rituals. He became very demanding and pressured me into taking different pictures almost every day! He said that if I didn't, he would tell Slaanesh to destroy me! I don't think I have ever been so scared in my whole life as I was of Kyle and Slaanesh.

During this time, I was missing a lot of school and instead of studying for my A levels, I was going round my friends houses and getting drunk. On one particular occasion, myself and two of my friends decided to miss afternoon lessons and go back to one of my friends houses. His parents were out and so we decided to play a game of poker. The idea was, that every time we lost a round, we had to have a shot of vodka. It turned out that I was awful at poker and the more I lost, the more I drank and so became extremely drunk. I can remember playing the last round and I lost again. I was so drunk that my two friends had to open my mouth to pour the vodka in as I was no longer in control. The next thing I remember was being violently sick on his bed and having to lie down. When I woke up, Slaanesh was in control. I was naked from the waist down and my friends penis was in my mouth. After that, he proceeded to rape me. I couldn't do anything, I couldn't even move or speak as I was too drunk.

The next thing I recall is my sister being phoned and my dad coming to pick me up from Robert's house. He took me straight to the local hospital where I had to stay overnight and have my stomach pumped.

My life was spiraling out of control and I needed to do something about it.

I had no where else to turn to and so I turned to Jesus. I prayed to him to help me and to take the demons away. I also told Chris what had been happening and he told Jay. It was time to put a stop to all this and to finish the deliverance. We booked our flights to America that night and flew out a few months later.

The night before flying out to Dallas, I was attacked by the demons severely. They made me vomit and shake uncontrollably as they did not want me to meet with Jay and Elizabeth.

We took the seven hour flight to Dallas Fort Worth airport and Jay met us there. He took us to our hotel room and left us to get some rest before meeting for prayer in the evening. I felt very ill and didn't want to be there at all. I kept saying to Chris, 'lets just go home', but of course, we couldn't. We were there for the whole two weeks.

I cannot recall much of our time in America. I remember the day time when Jay and Elizabeth and Jay's mother took us out visiting places, but when it comes to the deliverance, I can't remember a thing. Again, I was in a coma like state and will have to rely on Chris and Jay to tell the story.

> *A young lady from London, England traveled last year to meet my wife and I for prayer — to find liberation from the evil spirits that have tormented her for years. My heart broke over the life she had lived — drug abuse, self mutilation, severe abuse, mental torment, Satanism, occult activity, communion with demons, and other evils. Though the evil*

was immense the grace of God was extended, in a loving manner, to this young lady.

For seven straight days the body of Christ battled the forces of darkness in the power of the Holy Spirit. We held nightly prayer / exorcism sessions for this young lady at the beautiful Mt. Olive Free Methodist Church in Dallas. For seven straight days, some of the sessions lasting late into the night, we battled the forces of darkness, each night evil spirits were cast out — many very powerful spirits that resisted (but not for long as God's power overcame their strength).

The demonic powers would place this young lady in a trance like state and demons spoke out of her, often times in a strange voice unlike hers (some even growled and acted like an animal). Most of the time her eyes had rolled in the back of her head, we saw only the white — the demon looking at us.

Each night, it seemed as though we were dealing with stronger spirits then the night before but God was merciful and allowed us to minister to this young lady in love as we asked her to repent of the sins that allowed the various evil spirits access to her life. She did and God forgave her.

The evil powers named themselves and gave us the spiritual right they held unto in the lady's life. This allowed us to systematically demolish the various strongholds that the demonic beings that built over the years. Glory to Jesus Christ of Nazareth.

The body of Christ at Mt. Olive Free Methodist Church stood in their Christ given authority and earnestly prayed for this woman's deliverance. For 30 hours, over seven days, we battled and battled. We persevered. But we were not alone

— God's Holy angels arrived to the church and assisted us in battled. Allow me to explain...

Often times the demons would completely knock the young lady to the ground (even cause her to crawl around like an animal at times). In each instance, we commanded the angels to pick her up off the ground and in each instance the angels listened and obeyed our commands. The angels literally, without the aid of any human assistance, picked the body of the lady up off the ground and placing her in a position where we could minister to her. What an awesome display of God's goodness and power! Many angels showed up and one angel actually appeared to the lady in the sanctuary.

The angels assisted in also restraining the demons, binding them, and holding them (as there were a number of times the demons attempted to force the young lady outside of the church). In several instances the demons did cause her to leave the church only for the angels to bring her back in by our commands in the name of Jesus.

What a good God we serve as He allows us to minister alongside His angels for His glory.

Then the finale was a few nights ago. For hours we battled and battled the evil forces that remained. Anointing oil, the Word of God (the sword of the Spirit), holy water, the sacred symbols of the cross, the blood of Christ, and consecrated materials were utilized to drive out the demons.

I also equipped the saints that were present. I wanted them to be a part of the work of the Holy Spirit, so I invited many of them to cast out the demons in the name of Jesus. I gently instructed the saints on how to minister to the young lady and they exercised their faith and their were RESULTS — evil spirits were cast out of the body in the name of Christ, our eternal God.

One of the saints present was a 10 year old boy who loves Jesus. He commanded two of the demons out. Other saints also participated and more evil spirits were cast out. This isn't about Jay Bartlett — it's about the body of Christ working together for the glory of God alone. The church was so encouraged and now desires to assist others whom are demonized.

Toward the end of our session the senior pastor and I dealt with the last evil spirit who threatened to kill me. It was an intense war — but the last evil spirit was driven out. Fifty-seven evil spirits were expelled, sins were renounced, emotional healing took place, and the young lady was instantly healed of various physical aliments.

Whilst we were in America, Jay managed to take away a lot of demons from me. I was also healed of chest pains and breathing problems. Jay also spoke to a lot of the personalities within me and brought healing to them from the abuse they had suffered over the years. Towards the end of the two weeks we spent in Dallas, Jay married Chris and I and we had a party in the church afterwards to celebrate my healing and our marriage. We became very good friends with Jay and Elizabeth and it was lovely to be married by him. We were due to be married officially in Prague in February of the next year and so when we arrived home from Dallas, the preparations started.

We travelled to Prague a week before getting married and were married in a beautiful church on the 9th February 2007. It was a beautiful, bright, but very cold day and the wedding reception was held in a local restaurant. Most of our family made it to our big day and we had a great time. This was one of the happiest days of my life. My dress was amazing and I felt like a princess as we stood on Charles Bridge having our photos taken. Even some of the tourists stopped to take pictures of us. I was on top of the world.

After the wedding, I moved into our newly built apartment in North London with Chris. I found this extremely hard. I moved away from all my family and friends and found it very difficult to settle in. Chris' sister Wendy helped me move my belongings from Margate to London and some strange things happened that day.

I finished my last day at work and went home to pack the rest of my things. It was quite a warm evening, but my house was icy cold. You could see your breath when you breathed in my bedroom, it was that cold! This, I thought was strange as my dad had the central heating on in the house. When Wendy arrived, she got to the front door and before pressing the bell our fire and burglar alarm went off! My cat went crazy and darted from one room to the other as if possessed. Things were going crazy and we couldn't stop them! Other strange things happened such as weird noises were coming from my bedroom and strange smells permeated the air. All of these things, I believe, were the work of the devil and his demons telling me they weren't ready to let me go. The demons that were in my dad's house didn't want me to move away, as they would have lost all hold over and control of me. By moving to London, I had made them angry.

I was sad to be leaving home but happy at the same time to be starting my new married life with Chris. I had a new job, and a new husband. What could possibly go wrong? I was about to find out.

Over the next few weeks, I was naturally home sick. I longed to be back at home with my dad and sister and I missed my old job. However, Chris and I started our new lives by going on honeymoon to Tenerife. It was a brilliant holiday, however Chris' granddad passed away whilst we were there and so on my first day in my new job, Chris had to go to the funeral.

The night before, I felt sick. I was worrying about starting my new job in London and I hated being away from my dad. I didn't sleep at all that night and kept having panic attacks where I couldn't breathe and kept shaking uncontrollably. I missed my friends and family and wanted to go home.

Over the next few months, my panic attacks got worse and I ended up having to see a doctor, who put me on some medication to help with the attacks. I was also put on an anti depressant to help with my mood as I was feeling so low. Things weren't going great, until one day, Chris and I had some great news. It was July 2007 and I found out that I was pregnant with our first child, due in April 2008. We were both over the moon but very scared as it was all happening so fast! We desperately wanted children but didn't expect it to happen so soon after getting married. However, this is what God had planned for us and so we got very excited as the months went past. We found out in December that we were having a boy. This was fantastic news! I went out nearly every weekend to buy lots of little boys clothes and we decorated his bedroom blue and white with a stencil of a hippo on the wall by his cot. I finished work at the beginning of March 2008 and we were now ready for our little one to enter the world.

My contractions started on the Thursday morning and Chris' mother came over to be with me in case anything happened whilst he was at work. During the day they got worse and more frequent and so I phoned Chris to get him to come home from work early.

That evening the pain was so bad and I phoned my older sister who was living the other side of London. She came over and we called the hospital. By 11pm we arrived at the hospital and my waters broke in the car park! This shocked me so much, as I don't think it had sunk in that I was having the baby! I was taken to the labour suite and by 12:07am on the 4th April 2008 Koby-Lee was born weighing 7lbs 1oz. He was beautiful, but I couldn't hold him straight away. The midwife gave him to Chris to hold and I just watched, totally amazed and very scared at the thought of having this child to look after. He was so small and vulnerable. How could I possibly look after such a precious little one?

After taking a shower, I held Koby-Lee for the first time and fed him. Looking into his little face, I felt so much love for him. I wanted to protect him from everything. He was never going to suffer the way I had as a child, I would make sure of that.

The next day, Chris' family arrived to see the new baby. They picked him up and cuddled him and I immediately felt sick. I kept thinking, 'get off my baby.' The more they cuddled him and took pictures of him, the worse I felt. I even stayed in the bathroom for a while crying and being sick at the thought of people touching and holding my baby. I felt awful. My depression had started. From that moment, until Koby turned eight months old, I was a wreck. I couldn't eat or sleep and kept vomiting every time someone held him. Every time he cried I would cry and couldn't pick him up. Chris had to do everything. I was convinced that he was going to be taken away from me. I thought that Chris' mum wanted to take him from me and that I would never see him again.

My deliverance was not yet complete and so when Koby was 7 months old we went back to America for another deliverance session with Jay.

We stayed in the church for two weeks and many more demons were driven out in Jesus name. I will allow Chris to explain.

> Over a period of five sessions a total of 86 demons were taken away from Nataley.
>
> Prior to Nataley arriving in America for ministry, Jay received emails from a blasphemy spirit within her. This spirit, under the power of the Holy Spirit identified the following demons that were resident.
>
> 6 Blasphemy
> 2 Curse. These came from father through a curse as he curses. Inflicting Rosie.
> 1 Baby sex. This was a generational spirit (2 generations) that came from Nataley's mother.
> 33 Pleasure. These demons came in through sin. They entered at the age of 14 through looking at internet pornography.
> 100 Anger
> 100 Hate
> 1 Lucifer
> 1 Basilisk – A generational spirit which was passed to Nataley from her mother through the occult. This spirit originated in Nataley's Great-grandfather.. Her Grandfather did not know that he had it.
> 4 Incest
> 2 Psycho
> 67 Witchcraft
> 1 Dark Angel
> 16 Nightmare. These spirits were also affecting Nataley's son Koby- Lee. All Cast out of Nataley and Koby- Lee.

1 Mute. This spirit was affecting Darren. It was cast out and Darren now talks with an American accent!

Parts of Nataley identified

Through the ministry sessions a definitive list of alters were identified and communicated with.

1st Generation alters
- *Sad Nataley (has 11 spirits – 1 cast out) – Came about when Koby-Lee was born*
- *Charlie – strongest personality age 3*
- *Ark (baby) – now united with Nataley*
- *Darren – Age 6*
- *Lily – was trapped and an angel came to `her and unlocked her so that she is free to communicate. Lily is age 5 and is Darren's sister*
- *Rosie Ann – Age 14 has demons*
- *Maisie – Age 10 (Shared with sister Susan)*
- *Lenny – Age 8*
- *Natty – Age 14. Natty is Rosie Ann's twin sister*

Ancestral (generational) alters

- *David – Ancestral – from uncle*
- *Julie – Ancestral – From mother*
- *Kealy – Ancestral – From mother (see later note)*

Specific notes from the ministry sessions

The Homosexual Demon

This demon was a strongman and was guarding Ark within Nataley.

Homosexual had no right to Nataley, it's main purpose was to upset Ark. It appeared to Ark as a man in order to abuse him. This abuse lasted consistently for several years Ark came about due to sexual abuse of Nataley at age 14 months.

Homosexual was cast out. Ark was released and came to full consciousness within the ministry. Ark knew very few words and acted as a little baby should act. When he came to consciousness he cooed and looked around, Chris gave him a soft toy to hold which he clung on to as if it was his greatest possession. In fact because Ark had been locked up for so long it was his only possession. When the demons that were holding Ark came out, his job was done and wanted to return to Nataley's core personality. Ark was healed and made one with Nataley. When Koby – Lee was a young baby, some of the personalities mistook him for Ark which gives some indication as to what Ark looked like physically.

Before being cast out, Homosexual named the six strongmen holding Nataley, including the secret one intimated by the blasphemy spirit in the original email.

The strongmen are:

1. Beast
2. Charken Baby (x121)
3. Homosexual

4. Lucifer
5. Dark Angel
6. Charken – the secret strongman located in the mind.

Homosexual also stated the following:

A tracking device was placed in Nataley's wrist by Charken. It was put in by Doris (Children of God cult member) when Nataley was aged 5. It was inserted in the mouth and was still activated. The device was put in there so the cult (Doris) could find Nataley to send more demons into her.

Sarah, Doris's daughter has been used to locate Nataley through the internet community Facebook so that she will do the same stuff as the Children of God cult (Incest).

The chip was from Anton LaVey. Another Satanic cult gave it to Children of God. The chip was being held by Charken and Charken baby.

Homosexual was then cast out.

Basilisk

This demon reported to Charken Baby and to Beast. Basilisk was a generational spirit brought in through the Occult. It originated in Nataley's Great Grandfather, although future generations were unaware of it's presence. It came in to bring pain and mental illness through the generational line. Its specific job was to inflict neck pain on it's host. This demon was keeping Nataley in severe bondage. Basilisk was cast out.

Morph

The spirit had an arrogant personality and stated that it was there to do whatever it wanted. It was brought in by a generational curse on the mothers side through a Satanic blood ritual. It has been present for five generations and reported to Charken Baby.

Within the church where the ministry was taking place was a room set aside for deliverance ministry with a large wooden cross on the wall. As both myself and Nataley were staying within the Church access to this room was easy. One morning I noticed that a hooded jumper with what looked like blood stains had been draped across the cross in the deliverance room so that the cross could not be seen.

Within that night's ministry session, Morph admitted to covering the cross in the deliverance room. He stated that Charken Baby had given the order.

With outrage that the Cross of Jesus had been defiled by a demon in such a way, Jay ordered the angels of God to take Morph from the main Chapel, down the corridor to the deliverance room. We saw as the demon struggled within Nataley's body and struggled as the angels marched the demon to the room. Once there, the angels made Morph take the jumper down. It refused and was severely reprimanded by the angel's swords. Once Morph had been weakened it threw the jumper on the floor and stood face to face with the cross.

Jay then ordered Morph to kneel at the foot of the cross and touch it as a sign of being defeated by the power of God.

After a struggle, as Nataley violently shook, Morph touched the cross and stated that it was burning while the angels held it's hands on the cross.

Following this, Morph was take back to the main chapel and cast out of Nataley's body.

Vile (Formerly known as Koby-Lee)

The Vile spirit originally took the name Koby-Lee until reprimanded and the name changed to vile.

Vile came into Sad Nataley due to a generational curse on the mother's side. It came in after Nataley's mother's abortion. Vile causes rejection of the baby and the unwillingness to hold a baby at birth. This was activated when Nataley gave birth to Koby-Lee. For months Nataley could not hold him and suffered with post natal depression and a severe feeling of rejection towards her son.

Before Vile was cast out it stated that there were ten other spirits within Sad Nataley and named hate and Schizophrenia (the most powerful). Both these spirits were bound but not cast out.

Hallows Eve

On Halloween Jay Bartlett was speaking at the local Salvation Army centre and we went along to give him support. This demon entered Nataley because of a beast that appeared outside the Salvation Army on Halloween. The Halloween demon came off the flag pole, scratched Rosie Ann and entered.

Rosie Ann states that a grey creature came down from the sky while she was looking up outside the Salvation Army. Hallows eve was cast out the next evening.

Although Rosie Ann sees over ten demons she also sees and has experienced the light of God which makes her willing to carry out her own deliverance in order to help Nataley.

Charken and Charken Baby

Charken means to hunt and to multiply and was there because of Doris and the Children of god cult. Doris originally had Charken but was passed to Nataley through the sinful acts of the cult and Nataleys involvement in it. Although Charken was addressed in previous ministry sessions it was still yet to leave. Charken originated in America through Anton LaVey.

A control chip was placed within Nataley's right wrist by Doris. The right to the chip is Nataley and the cult involvement at age 5. Doris video taped the sexual acts for blackmail purposes. Charken stated that Doris still has the tape. Angels were despatched to destroy the tape.

196 seeds were placed in the body by the cult to enable the Charken Baby's to multiply. It was stated that 13 of the Charken Baby's were there because of the seeds. Charken Baby's were there to hurt Nataley.

Charken was there to bring the teachings of Children of God into Nataley's mind. The teaching of family of love (incest is OK).

Doris holds the chip. She now lives in Wales and Astral Projects to Nataley. Doris appears in Nataley's dreams wanting contact with Nataley.

The 196 seeds were destroyed by the applying of consecrated water which burned the seeds out and along with them 13 of the Charken baby's cast out. The lay lines and cords were broken to stop Doris Astral Projecting to Nataley. The tracking device was dissolved and destroyed.

Charken was finally cast out.

Sarah

There was one spirit called Sarah which was cast out. There was no right but was used for Sarah (Doris's daughter) to Astral Project to Nataley. Nataley was then advised to cut all communications through Facebook and mobile phone with Sarah to stop the door re opening.

Lucifer

This was a Strongman brought in by Nataley reading the Satanic Bible and by both Nataley and Rosie Ann looking at Occult websites. Lucifer was inflicting pain on Rosie Ann's mind in order to hurt her. Lucifer was cast out.

Lennie

Lennie is a human personality that is part of Nataley. He is age 8 and does not speak.

Lennie had one demon also named Lennie. This is a generational spirit brought in on the mothers side through a curse (I forbid you to speak) uttered by a family member. The generational curse brings in speech impediments.

Lennie spirit was there to lock the Lennie personality up and stop him talking. Lennie spirit was cast out and Lennie personality is free to talk although he is not heard from often.

Pleasure

33 pleasure spirits entered Nataley through looking at internet pornography at the age of 14. All were cast out.

Dark Angel

This was a strongman with no right. It was a generational spirit that has been around for six generations. Brought in from Nataley's fathers involvement in Freemasonry. Nataley affected because she wore the gloves, knows the handshakes and uses them when messing around. Dark angel enters people through this. Dark angel reports to no one and was cast out.

Nightmare

There were a total of 16 nightmare spirits within both Nataley and Koby-Lee.

Within the session the spirits were first of all cast out of Nataley and then out of Koby-Lee. Because Koby-Lee was not present at the session the spirits were cast out from a distance. I used my God given authority as the spiritual head of the household to cast them out from a distance. As they had no right to Koby-Lee, a group of angels were despatched to where he was and carried out a battle with the nightmare spirits and took them out of Koby-Lee's body.

Morken

There were two Morken spirits with the same rights. They entered at age 15 through a man that Nataley met through the Occult websites called Shaman Knight who was Astral Projecting to Nataley and using her body for Occultic purposes..

The Morken spirits work with Beast and both Morken spirits were cast out.

Mute

The Mute spirit was affecting Darren and had no rights to Nataley or Darren. The Mute spirit was cast out and Darren can now speak.

Brother

The Brother spirit was guarding Darren . it states that It was there to be friends with Darren and was sent by Beast. The Brother spirit was cast out and Darren was set free.

Kealy

Kealy is an ancestral personality and was originally in Julie (Nataley's mother) and sent to Nataley to take bad memories away. Kealy was trapped by four cancer spirits which were there because Julie suffered and was killed by cancer. The types of cancer present are lymphatic, lung and blood. The spirits were brought in by a spirit of disease.

Disease and the four cancer spirits have been bound but not cast out.

Another personality Julie was also previously in Nataley's mother.

Both have been sent by God to help Nataley at this time and when their job is done they will return to Julie.

Remaining strongmen

Nataley has been delivered of all of the Strongmen except Beast which was implanted into her at conception by the doctor that carried out the artificial insemination procedure. The doctor implanted Beast into her in order to make the perfect 'Devil child'.

List of demons taken away in this ministry session

6 Blasphemy
2 Curse

1 Baby sex
33 Pleasure
1 Lucifer (Strongman)
1 Basilisk
1 Dark Angel (Strongman)
16 Nightmare
1 Mute
1 Charken (Strongman)
1 Homosexual
1 Vile
1 Hallows Eve
1 Morph
13 Charken Baby
1 Sarah
1 Lucifer (Strongman)
1 Lennie
1 Morken
1 Mute
1 Brother

A total of 86 in this ministry session.

During this ministry session, the demon called beast revealed some very important information.

My mother had to have an operation in order to conceive. This operation was performed by a professor who was studying child birth at the time. Beast told us that this professor had demons and he put beast inside the egg that was to produce me. I was then conceived using this egg and beast entered my body whilst in the womb. He said that it was done on purpose in order to produce a child belonging to Satan that would destroy the church and deliverance ministry.

The professor was present at my birth and followed my progress until I was six years old. This is when beast was activated in me and started causing me all the problems.

Beast then went on to say how he could be cast out. The only way it could be done is to have my father renounce the curse on the egg and only he has the authority in Jesus as the child's father to cast the demon out. Of course, the demon knew that my father doesn't believe in any form of religion and so it would be impossible to cast the demon out. However, God will show us a way to get rid of the beast and I will be free of him.

Over time my depression got worse and so my doctor sent me to see a psychiatrist. He said I was probably suffering from post natal depression and he prescribed me some more anti depressants. My thought patterns changed and I began to be scared of every thing. I was convinced that people were trying to poison me and so I wouldn't eat food. When I went out, I thought that people were plotting against me and were going to stab me. It became very hard to travel on a bus as I wanted to attack people because I thought they were going to attack me first and that they were talking about me. I believed they new all about me and that the police were in a conspiracy against me.

I phoned my psychiatrist and told him what was happening. He sent a nurse straight round to see me and she contacted the hospital. I was so sick that I was either to be admitted to hospital, or have the Home Treatment Team round to visit me every day. I was assessed by this team and they agreed I could stay at home as I had a baby to look after. However, I was put on strong anti depressants and anti psychotic drugs and I was visited every day by a psychiatrist. I didn't understand what was happening to me and so began to self harm again. I would also see and hear things that weren't there such as voices and people. George was one of the people that I would see. He would tell me that the police were trying to get me and he would tell me that people were plotting against me. Of course, I was ill so I believed every word he said. He would even appear on the television and talk to me through the radio. This was the beginning of a very serious illness.

After about 3 weeks, the Home Treatment Team discharged me back to the community psychiatric team and I was seen every month by my psychiatrist and psychiatric nurse. The medication was working and I started to feel a lot better. My mood had gone back to almost normal and I wasn't having as many psychotic episodes. I decided to come off my medication. Big mistake. Things rapidly got worse again and the doctors didn't know exactly what was wrong with me.

I went to see my psychiatrist for a routine check up. I was feeling very low again and the voices in my head were getting worse. They convinced me that the best way to help myself was to die. So I told Dr Amos that I wanted to die and that I was going to kill my whole family. I told him that it would be nice for us to all die together and that I was going to tamper with the smoke alarms in our house so that we could die. I had a plan.

Dr Amos immediately referred me back to the Home Treatment Team and informed social services of what I had said. The next day, a doctor from the team and social services turned up on my door step. They said they were very concerned about me and what I had said and that they had to monitor me and my family as they believed we were at risk. They said that Koby was at risk from me and that they had to see him every week. I was also to be visited by the Home Treatment Team every other day and I was put back on my medication. I believe that if I hadn't cooperated, Koby may have been taken away from me and put into care there and then. I was very frightened. I loved Koby so much and couldn't bear to be away from him so I did what they said, I began to take my medication again.

Over the next few days, I started getting better again. It was Koby's first birthday and all the family came round for a party. We had a great day and Koby got lots of lovely presents. That night, we had some more great news. I was pregnant again! I was very happy but terrified at the same time. I would have to stop taking my medication and what if I got ill again? What if the depression and psychotic thoughts started again with this new child? I phoned the Home Treatment Team immediately and told them what had happened. They came round to see me and told me that I had to stop taking the medication straight away as it wasn't safe to take during pregnancy. I was very scared. Could we cope with another child and my illness? Social services were informed and a conference was planned to take place to decide what was best for Koby and our unborn child.

We attended the conference and my medical history was spoken about and how I had planned to kill the whole family. After a long discussion and reports read out by various professionals, it was decided that Koby and the unborn child would go on a child protection plan. This meant that I would have to be seen by a psychiatric nurse every other week and Koby was to be seen by a social worker and health visitor every 10 days. I was so upset. What had I done to my family? I hadn't abused Koby in any way at all and I loved him so much that it seemed so unfair that this was happening to me. They also wanted me to be assessed by a forensic team at the hospital to find out exactly what my illness was.

After the meeting my mood became very low again and because I wasn't taking any medication, the psychotic episodes increased. I was now convinced that someone had placed a metal detection device inside me and so I began to cut open my skin to get it out. I really thought that I could see it and so I ripped open my arm and pulled it out and destroyed it. The Home Treatment team were very worried.

The day that I went for my forensic examination, I was very scared. I didn't really know what to expect and I was told that it would take 3 hours! My older sister came to the hospital with me and waited outside. I sat round a table with two doctors and they asked me lots of questions. I was very honest with them and told them how I was feeling and what George was telling me. All the time I was in there, I could see George walking around outside by the window. They asked me what I was looking at and I told them that George didn't want me to go for the examination and he was waiting for me outside.

At the end of our discussion I had to do a questionnaire and look at pictures and tell them what I thought they looked like. I was also given coloured cubes to make models and patterns with. After a series of tests, I was allowed to go. I had been in there 3 and a half hours! I was very tired and drained and went home and slept for the whole afternoon.

A few weeks later I received a letter to say I had to go back to see the doctors again for another assessment. So I arrived at the hospital again and saw a consultant forensic psychiatrist. He was very scary looking and kept asking me lots of questions. After about an hour, he told me that he was going to write to my doctor and get me put on some different medication that was safe during pregnancy. I felt relieved. At least now I could stop worrying about being ill and start getting better. The consultant also told me what was wrong with me. He diagnosed me as having schizoaffective disorder which is a mixture of bi polar and schizophrenia. I was to take medication for the rest of my life, or else I would get sick again. I wasn't too happy at the thought of this as I hated taking medication and being labeled as mentally ill but at least now I could get better and concentrate on the arrival of our second child. I phoned the social worker and told him my diagnosis. He was a specialist in dealing with parents with mental illness and said that he thought that was what I had wrong with me and that it was good now that I had been properly diagnosed as the right medication would be given to me. I was put on anti depressants and anti psychotics and was told to take them every day and to this day, I still have to take them.

In August 2009 we found out that we were to have a little girl. We were so happy. I always wanted a little princess! I immediately went out and brought lots of pink things for our little princess. We redecorated Koby's bedroom so half was a builder with his tools and half were princesses. After the birth of Koby, I had gone back to work two days a week as a nursery nurse in the local nursery and I was due to go on maternity leave in October. We were now ready for our little girl to arrive!

Summer Jaye was born on the 28th November 2009 at about 3:47am. I say about this time as every thing happened so fast, we were unable to record the time. Allow me to explain.

I woke up at 3am on the Saturday morning with tummy ache. Chris told me to try and go to the toilet which I did. My tummy ache wouldn't go away and I tried to go back to sleep but couldn't. I then realized that I was having contractions. I went for a hot bath and when I got out, I started to bleed and the contractions were only about 2 minutes apart! Chris phoned the hospital and they told us to wait to come in until my waters had broken.

Only a few minutes later, I could feel my waters beginning to break. Chris' sister Celia was staying over that night and we woke her up to tell her what was happening. We then phoned my sister to tell her to meet us at the hospital as she was to be my birthing partner again.

The pain got so bad that I started to feel sick. Sitting on the toilet, I thought I was going to pass out with the pain! Celia stayed with me in the bathroom whilst Chris called for an ambulance. Whilst he was on the phone, the baby's head came out! I screamed and walked to the bedroom as she started to push herself out. I lay down on the bed and within 30 seconds, Summer had been born! It had only taken 45 minutes from when I woke up with tummy ache, to Summer arriving!

Chris prayed and asked angels to come and help bring Summer into the world. Charlie informed us afterwards that four angels had been sent by Jesus to help deliver her and that was the reason it went smoothly.

The paramedics arrived about 5mins later and Chris got to cut the cord. Koby woke up and saw the baby. He got very excited and gave her a kiss on the head.

The paramedics called my midwife and she came round straight away. She gave me an injection to give birth to the placenta and after about an hour, I was in the ambulance on my way to the hospital with our new little girl. Charlie was very excited about riding in an ambulance.

When we arrived at the hospital, the baby was checked over and we were told she weighed 5lbs 15ozs. She was so tiny! I had never seen a baby that small before! She was absolutely beautiful and looked like Koby. I cradled her in my arms and with a big smile on my face said 'I'm your mummy.' She slept all that day and so I managed to get some rest before she wanted feeding. Because she was under the child protection plan with social services and I was on medication, we had to stay in hospital over the weekend until a meeting took place to allow us to go home.

Arriving home was the best feeling in the world. We took our little girl into the house and she opened her eyes to have a look round. She looked at me and drifted off to sleep again. She looked so peaceful and content. I was so happy that my medication hadn't had any affect on her at all. She was a very happy and healthy little baby. Koby came home from nursery and gave Summer a big cuddle and a kiss.

After the birth of Summer, I was worried that I would suffer from post natal depression again. The midwives kept a very close eye on me and would visit every other day. Fortunately, I haven't suffered depression at all. I felt totally different with this birth and haven't had any signs of depression. I have had my ups and downs over the last month but that's to be expected looking after two young children. Some days I find harder than others but overall, life is good!

Summer is growing fast and doing really well. Koby is overall, very good with her. He has his moments like most children do, but he loves his little sister and is very protective of her. He likes to cuddle her and hold her and when she cries he gives her a dummy and her dolly. He is very sweet with her.

As for the deliverance sessions, they are still ongoing. A lot of work has been done but there is still more to do. Jay will be coming to London in the near future and will spend some time with us in prayer. We are also going to go over to Dallas at the end of the year to complete the work.

Our future plans are to move over to Dallas. Chris is looking for a job over there and we intend to look for a place to live at the end of the year. We believe God is telling us we need to be there to help Jay with his ministry and so I can help others who are suffering the way I did. I would love to meet with people who have gone through the same as me and to be able to help them, the way Jay has helped me over the last seven years.

We would also like to have more children in the future. We love children and would love to bring more into the world to love them and teach them about Jesus. We are already teaching Koby and Summer about Jesus and will show them the love of God every day. As they grow older, we hope they will follow him and help in the much needed ministry of deliverance.

References

Horrobin, P *Healing Through Deliverance*. Sovereign World Ltd, UK, 1994

Jacobs, C *Deliver Us From Evil*, Regal Books, UK 2001

Larson, B *Larson's New Book Of Cults*, Tyndale House Publishers Inc, USA,1989

Bartlett J, Exploring The Unknown, The Strange And The Supernatural, Xulon Press, USA, 2003

About the author

Christopher Ford is a member of the worldwide Salvation Army and attends the Church in North London.

He first felt called into Deliverance ministry in 1998 while on mission in Latvia. Since that time God has opened the door to ministry in the United Kingdom, Europe and North America.

For the past seven years Christopher has been studying Dissociative behaviour in a Christian Context. He is currently studying for a Bachelors Degree in Biblical Studies.

Christopher married Nataley in 2007 and they have been working together to fulfill Gods plan for their lives which includes full healing for Nataley and then the opportunity to share, help and deliver those who find themselves in similar circumstances.

Printed in Poland
by Amazon Fulfillment
Poland Sp. z o.o., Wrocław